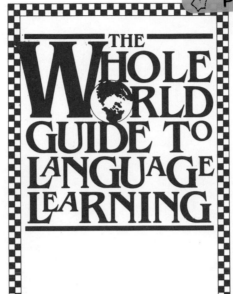

THE WHOLE WORLD GUIDE TO LANGUAGE LEARNING

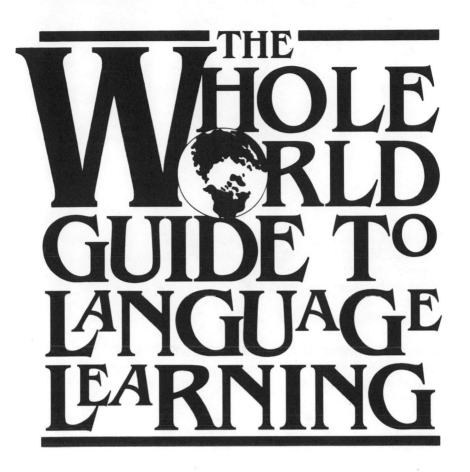

TERRY MARSHALL

intercultural press, inc.

Library of Congress Catalog No. 88-045727
ISBN 0-933662-75-0
Copyright © 1989 Terry Marshall
Published by Intercultural Press, Inc.
All rights reserved.
Printed in the United States of America.

For information, contact
Intercultural Press
P.O. Box 768
Yarmouth, Maine 04096

Library of Congress Cataloging-in-Publication Data

Marshall, Terry.
    The whole world guide to language learning: how to
live and learn any foreign language/by Terry Marshall.
        p.   cm.
    Bibliography: p.
    Includes index.
    ISBN 0-933662-75-0
    1.   Language and languages—Study and teaching.
2.   Communicative competence.   I.   Title.
P51.M355   1989
418'.007—dc20

88-45727

CIP

To Leslie and Shawn,

in hopes that our experiences

will enhance your ability

to appreciate other cultures and other languages.

TABLE OF CONTENTS

Preface

This book has its roots in the Philippines. In 1965, after ten weeks of intensive training in Tagalog, the Peace Corps sent my wife and me to Tacloban City, Leyte, where people speak not Tagalog but Waray-Waray. On our own we struggled to a passable speaking ability in our new language.

More than a dozen years later, as codirectors of Peace Corps programs in Solomon Islands, my wife and I set out to train a group of married couples who would live in different language-speaking areas. Each language was unwritten. No training courses or language teachers existed, and we set in motion the rudiments of the approach advocated in this book. One volunteer went on to write the first dictionary ever in the Tolo language.

This book is the manual we needed those many years ago. Along the way, many people helped make it possible. A few should be singled out.

David Hoopes, senior editor of Intercultural Press, found, in wading through my unsolicited first manuscript, nuggets enough to undertake publication.

Ann Marshall and Judy Carl Hendrick, in reading draft after draft, made innumerable suggestions that improved the book.

Donald Larson, Susan Crowley, Bob Crowley, Arthur Rodger and John Gaevin read and commented on various early drafts.

Through the years, our own mentors enriched our lives as they guided us into their own languages and cultures. A special thanks to Guillerma Villacorte, Palo, Leyte, Philippines; Alma Aletin, Tacloban City, Leyte, Philippines; Lupita Sanchez, Cuernavaca, Mexico; and Carolyn Siota and Francis Labu, Honiara, Solomon Islands.

Terry Marshall

One

Settling In:
Where Do I Go from Here?

Imagine that the long-awaited day has arrived. Not only are you "in-country," you have moved into what will be your home for the next year or two. That first-blush newness of arrival has become memory: the chaos of an unfamiliar airport, that first taxi or bus ride, the new smells, the initial anxiety of a new destination.

You have settled in, at least physically. You have moved from the hotel into your new "family's" home, an apartment, a house. You have made your first visits to the major sights: the marketplace and plaza, the cathedral, the town statues, the nearest beach and historic markers. You have tasted the local delicacy, washed it down with the local brew, exchanged pleasantries with your new coworkers or classmates and the neighborhood kids. And you have discovered how ill-prepared you are to carry on normal daily conversations.

You are not alone. It is a challenge faced by thousands of Americans each year. Your opportunity to live overseas may have come suddenly. Amid preparations for moving, winding up work and personal affairs, you have had no time to study a foreign language. You may be a spouse, uprooted when your husband or wife's employer decided work overseas must begin immediately. Skilled language students are not immune: you may find your straight-A classroom performance didn't prepare you to crowd up to the window and buy postage stamps or chat with neighbors about what you are doing in their country. Even if you studied in an intensive Peace Corps-type training program, you find that folks on the street spray words faster than a record on the wrong speed. They slur words, drop syllables. You speak clearly, but folks can't understand you.

On the other hand, maybe you are the exception. You speak the local language well enough to carry out your daily routine and perform your job, or are one of those gifted individuals who picks up languages without effort.

If, however, you are like most of us, if you

- find yourself living in a community where people speak a language you have never heard, let alone never studied; or
- have the basics, but find you can communicate only with language teachers; or
- are well on your way to mastering the language, but haven't yet become fluent, this book is for you.

Our goal for language learning is *communicative competence*. It's a simple goal: to be able to speak to, understand, and be understood by native speakers.

It sounds deceptively simple, communicative competence. It's strikingly different from the goals of many language programs. The aim is not to analyze the language, explain its grammatical structure, or hear lectures on such topics as the indicative use of subjective past participles in action clauses. It's not to memorize grammatical rules, manipulate lists of verbs, or sit through hours of conjugation drills.

Our goal is to communicate—effectively, efficiently, comfortably— with folks who speak the language. It means learning not only words, phrases, and sentences, but the cultural components of language—the social rules; the signs, gestures, and other nonverbal cues by which people communicate; the context in which words take on meaning.

If you share this goal with us, this book is for you.

MAKING IMMERSION WORK FOR YOU

In living abroad, you have taken a key step toward foreign language proficiency: native speakers, speaking naturally, surround you.

If you had a chance to study at all, however, you have found that despite your formal classes, training program, or self-study, you are not yet fluent.

Don Larson, a linguist with a distinguished background in language teaching in the Third World, reminds us that after formal classes come to an end, your learning must continue. "The school must therefore help the student to become a learner, to follow a different pattern: learners tapping the resources of knowers."[1] Yet, most courses fall into a standard pattern in which students study routines set for them by their teachers.

Living overseas verifies Larson's observation. You find yourself a learner as well as an expatriate. Without formal language class, though, you lack direction for your learning. Suddenly you must be a self-directed learner, a role for which you have not been trained.

Our message here is simple: you can greatly improve your language learning prospects (and better understand the culture and people of the country in which you are living) if you personally assume responsibility for your own language learning.

Unfortunately, as thousands of Peace Corps volunteers, business people, government workers, and study-abroad students can testify, living abroad merely provides an opportunity to learn. It does not guarantee language proficiency.

Immersion in a different culture sets the stage for language learning. For maximum benefit, however, you need an individual learning program which systematically taps the resources available in the community. Language learning, even when you are immersed in a native-speaking environment, will flourish best when not left to chance.

You can become fluent without formal classes or teachers by concentrating on your own needs rather than on performing for a language instructor. To do that, you need a framework which

1. provides direction for your language learning,

2. focuses your learning on areas of personal interest, and

3. systematically prepares you to deal with more complex language usage.

This introductory chapter outlines such a method. Subsequent chapters provide detailed recommendations for implementing your own language learning program. But first, let us place language learning in its proper cultural context.

THE CULTURAL CONTEXT OF LANGUAGE LEARNING

Living abroad is exhilarating. We make new friends; discover new sights, sounds, tastes, smells; see firsthand events, places, art works, historical and natural monuments we have only read about or seen on television. We plunge into different patterns of living, probe common events from new perspectives, challenge our assumptions about what is "natural" and "right."

Immersion in another culture provides much more than the setting for language learning. It serves as the context for an intense experience in cultural learning and personal growth. We learn about other peoples, gain insight into cultural and historical identities, priorities, and values different from our own. We gain, as much as anything else, a deeper understanding of ourselves as individuals and as members of a particular culture and nationality group.

Living as a foreigner is not all good times, of course. We become frustrated and perplexed when people misunderstand us and we fail to understand them; when our work seems to bring no result; when "simple" things go awry—mail arrives late; when grocery shopping consumes an entire morning; when the office telephone still hasn't been connected; when the prearranged taxi fails to show; when the bus stops on the "wrong" corner and we miss it; when the bed promised by the host organization comes a month late. We feel lonely, missing old friends, familiar sights and ways of doing things, and accustomed foods and leisure activities. We fall prey to illness or disease.

Living abroad can be stressful as we encounter cultural differences at deeper and deeper levels. We experience the uncertainty involved in deciphering unfamiliar cues, in coping with unfamiliar behaviors, in attempting to adjust to new ways of doing things.

Some days we wonder why we came. At other times, we rejoice that we have been so fortunate to experience life anew. Every day we are reminded that differences between ourselves and our hosts include not only language, but a complex pattern of beliefs, values, and activities that we call culture. Sometimes we fail to communicate because language differences impede us. At other times, we find the right words, but realize that something beyond language is at work.

The pursuit of communicative competence using the techniques recommended in this book takes place in the context of learning and adapting to living in another culture. The better you understand the language, the easier it will be to understand the cultural milieu about you. But the demands of your cultural experiences will sometimes seem to be barriers to your spending the time and energy needed to pursue language learning as intensely as is needed to become a fluent speaker.

Recognize the cultural context of your language learning. Expect to cope not only with a new language but also with the personal emotional challenges of living abroad.

LEARNING STYLE AND LANGUAGE STUDY

In recent years, linguists and language professionals have made great gains in language-teaching methodology. A host of different approaches have been developed based on experience and research into varied learning styles.

Traditional language teaching rested on the study of grammar. As language professionals realized that one doesn't necessarily learn to speak through grammar translation, speaking and listening exercises became common. More recently, researchers have looked not only at techniques of instruction but also at the instructional atmosphere as important components of good language training. Approaches have been advocated which emphasize long periods of listening before one begins to speak, physical response to words so as to tie language to action, reduction of stress for the learner through relaxation techniques, strong peer support and cooperation among fellow language learners, and inductive learning.[2]

Effective language learning involves more than learning words, phrases, and sentence structures. It is an interactive process involving language, culture, personality. Activities which work for one individual may not be effective for another. Effective language learning thus must rest not only upon particular learning techniques, but also on those techniques which are meaningful to you as an individual learner.

The recommendations for field-based language learning advocated in *The Whole World Guide to Language Learning* are based on a notion we call *in situ* exploration, or more simply, learning in place, that is, where the language is spoken. This method lets you direct your own learning. The approach is eclectic—it recognizes that specific objectives, particular activities, and learning exercises must mesh with the learning style which best fits you. As a learner, you must consider our recommendations with a self-analytical eye. Ask yourself, "How best do I learn?" "What kinds of activities best fit my preferred style as a learner?" "How can I use these suggestions to take advantage of my experience and strengths as a learner?"

The in situ approach is broad enough to accommodate a variety of learning styles. Let's take a look at it.

THE LEARNING CYCLE: A KEY TO SELF-DIRECTED LEARNING

In reality, only rarely do individuals have the tenacity (and need) to study foreign language entirely on their own. Most of us believe we need teacher direction. We feel lost without classes, books, someone who knows if we are correct or not. We need structure.

In conventional language study, structure is imposed by grammar. One studies language that is correct according to recognized rules.

Language classes follow grammatical structures, and students are introduced to new vocabulary and increasingly complex ideas as the class proceeds.

Recall your first language class. You memorized words and proper sentences. You learned that some things are correct and others incorrect. You started with present tense, moved on to past tense, etc. Your teacher told you what to do.

By contrast, people working in foreign settings and learning in situ have the opportunity and sometimes the need to approach language learning differently. They can draw upon the community and the expertise of a wide range of native speakers. (This is particularly true for people working overseas in remote areas where "exotic" languages are spoken and formal instruction impossible, as is often the case, for instance, with Peace Corps volunteers, missionaries, anthropologists, and linguists.) The community becomes the teacher.

From such situations comes a different structure for language learning: the learning cycle.

Structure in the learning cycle differs sharply from traditional language instruction. With it, you follow a logical learning process based on your own needs rather than on a linguistic analysis of the language.

The learning cycle recognizes that your key task as an on-site language learner is to decide what to learn and the order in which to learn it. The learning cycle answers the common problem of overseas language learners: "I don't know enough about the language to know what to do next!" You do need structure, but structure of a different sort, a structure which gives alternatives for learning what you believe you need to know to reach the language goals you have set for yourself.

The learning cycle organizes your learning process. In brief, using the cycle, you do the following:

1. **Decide** what to learn for the day; for example, a beginning explanation of yourself as a language learner and a request for assistance: "I want to learn to speak [Pijin]. This is all I can say. Thank you for listening!"

The decision of exactly what to learn, of course, is based on goals which you set for yourself. In the above case, the goal is mastery of phrases needed simply to begin talking with people in your new setting.

2. **Prepare**, with the help of a native-speaking helper or mentor, the desired conversation in the target language. For the above example, we come up with "*Mi nao trae fo lanim Pijin blong Solomone, ia. Hem nao evri samting wea mi nao save long hem. Taggio tumas fo herem toktoko blong mi, ia.*"

3. **Practice** speaking and listening to the lesson and various responses to it with the mentor until you can express fluently the desired phrases and understand likely responses with ease.

4. **Communicate** the learned message to other native speakers by going into the community, finding people, and speaking to them. Sometimes you are accompanied by a mentor; at other times you will venture out alone.

5. **Evaluate** your progress and the lesson's usefulness by discussing it with the mentor, modifying the phrases as necessary, and practicing the revised passage as needed.

The cycle then begins anew.

Actual lessons developed using the cycle will mature in complexity as you develop proficiency. An early lesson will be as simple as the one above. Later lessons may elicit community members' thoughts on various subjects or prompt discussion of community life, or language, or world views, or man's relation to his fellow man, or whatever.

Regardless of how a passage is used or modified, however, the principles remain the same: (1) decide; (2) prepare; (3) practice; (4) communicate; (5) evaluate.

The learning cycle assumes the presence of a native-speaking community, the continuing help of local mentors, and the absence of formal language classes or training. Since most language learning must ultimately take place outside the formal classroom, mastery of the learning cycle approach provides the structure for continued learning.

If, on the other hand, you are enrolled in a formal language class, the learning cycle provides a natural supplement to your formal classroom work.

An in situ approach implies three fundamental concepts which differ from more traditional language instruction: (1) the genuine dominance of speaking and listening goals; (2) the role of language instructor as guide and evaluator rather than teacher; and (3) the involvement of a native-speaking community as the primary role model for language use.

The first of these concepts is straightforward: when learning in situ, emphasis is upon the practical, particularly being able to understand spoken language, respond to it, and speak to others. Some reading and writing may be useful, but the emphasis is on survival skills—reading signs, notices, menus; filling out forms, writing simple notes, etc.—as opposed to writing formal compositions or reading literature, goals which dominate conventional language instruction.

The second and third concepts merit further discussion.

THE INSTRUCTOR'S NEW ROLE:
FROM TEACHER TO GUIDE

In traditional language study, teachers dominate the classroom. They decide the topics for study. They choose the order, content, and teaching methods. They are the model whose pronunciation, rhythm, and mastery students emulate.

Once you are overseas, you still need someone to help you learn. But rather than a teacher, look for a *mentor*. A mentor is a native speaker (not necessarily a classroom teacher) who agrees to help you systematically learn the local language. A good mentor will guide you and evaluate your progress. Your mentor will help you decide what to learn and introduce you to other community members. Your relationship with your mentor will be a special one; very likely, you will become friends, coworkers, fellow learners as well as mentor and learner.

Your mentor will guide, lead, cajole, direct you. And you will have a reciprocal teaching role—to help her develop and use those methods which best fit your learning style. With her help you will learn to

- paraphrase: develop appropriate texts in the locally used vernacular (texts drawn from your joint effort to visualize a likely situation, rather than from direct translation of your English sentences into proper formal usage);
- construct dialogues: create realistic, locally accepted speech patterns which become the basis for your lessons;
- conduct drills: supervise the practice that brings oral fluency and adds variety to your learning;
- use cultural cues to support your language learning;
- create simulations: practice exercises, skits, and role plays that prepare you to deal with real-life situations.

Your mentor becomes your key conduit to language fluency. Mentor and learner enjoy a sharing relationship, one expanded by an increasing circle of native speakers in your community.

The mentor role, hints on selecting and working with mentors, and language learning techniques that mentors can use are discussed in detail in chapter 4.

COMMUNITY AS CLASSROOM:
IN SITU EXPLORATION

The notion of drawing on a community as your teacher is simple: planned interaction with native speakers outside a classroom can speed your language learning, provide immediate relevance for the words and phrases you study, and demonstrate that language is meaningful as a tie to the local community.

In theory, community exploration comes easily once you are overseas. These days, if you are with an agency such as the Peace Corps, the training program **not** conducted in an in-country setting, or at least without a home stay, is the exception. If you have enrolled in a study abroad program, you will likely live in a dormitory, with a family, or in an apartment surrounded by members of the local community. If you are a professional employed abroad, or the spouse of one, you may have to be more deliberate in creating community exploration opportunities.

Even with home or dormitory stays, you may fail to capitalize fully on the language learning potential: presence in an environment conducive to language study does not **automatically** result in language mastery. You need planned activities based on community interchange to use fully the excellent opportunities which in-country language study presents.

In situ exploration involves you in the native-speaking community at two levels. First, mentorships link you in a continuing relationship with native speakers. Frequently, mentors are fellow students, coworkers, "family" members (if you live with a local family). Additionally, you will develop community mentors as well—community men and women who simply become intrigued by the idea of helping you learn their language. We found in the South Pacific, for instance, that elderly persons, children, and young professionals enjoyed being mentors to Peace Corps volunteers.

Second are the more casual relationships which develop with others in the community, such as language informants: persons whose interests, positions, or accessibility expand your learning in different contextual areas. In the South Pacific, elders and women who gather in particular locations open vital windows to village life and language. Other language informants include artisans and the experts in important local tasks, such as canoe-making, leaf-weaving, fishing, etc.

Some informants will be those you meet in local shops, front yards, the offices of the organizations to which you belong. They may be host country students or host families if you are a student. Others will be strangers, people you meet in the street, at meetings, or social events.

The in situ idea assumes that language-learning activities will be carefully designed, practiced, executed, and evaluated. It assumes that the learner-mentor relationship is carefully developed. We do not advocate sending you into a community to "hang out"; nor do we expect you to get together with a native speaker and magically learn his or her language. The following chapters describe how to make these relationships work.

In summary, this book advocates language learning based on learner independence and community involvement. This method—in situ exploration—proposes involving native-speaking mentors, who, with a five-step learning cycle, help guide your language learning, drawing effective language usage from the local community.

The following chapters explain the concepts in detail and provide specific activities to launch you on your way.

[1]Larson, Don, *Barefootnotes* I, I (September-October 1984), p. 1.
[2]The literature on language teaching methodology is extensive. Because *The Whole World Guide* addresses language learners, we will avoid discussing various theoretical approaches. For an introduction to the topic, see Lafayette and Strasheim, p. 567-74.

Two

Independence:
Creating and Using a Daily Learning Cycle

The end of a language course can be exhilarating. It means relief from tedious drilling, memorization, and the stress of listening, speaking, and concentrating on a different language. It brings to an end teacher-imposed structures and unbending schedules.

Unfortunately, your new-found freedom will be short-lived if you want or need to continue learning the language and use it for practical purposes. A structured process is required, though not necessarily the same kind you used in the classroom.

Too often, structure in language learning means a formal class-room. An in situ approach provides the structure that is necessary for language learning, but without the inflexibility of a formal classroom.

An effective individual language program must have **a structured process which organizes your learning**. You can master a language more quickly if your study continues systematically. Though some people seem to pick up languages by just being exposed to them, most of us need planned activities, organized procedures, and regular study; other-wise, we quickly reach a plateau where our progress stops. Without constant practice, we gradually lose whatever basic skills we have developed in our formal classes.

A structured individual language program also needs **detailed**

learning activities and study techniques. Self-directed learning falters most often because learners don't know what specific activities are of greatest help to them. You have to **do something** to learn another language; you can't just lean back and absorb it. Suggestions, hints, and exhortation help, but without detailed learning objectives and activities— the specific words, phrases, sentences, structures that a traditional language class provides—most of us find language learning on our own too difficult. We resort to osmosis, at best an erratic and fickle teacher.

This chapter shows how you can direct your own language learning with the help of the **daily learning cycle**.

The daily learning cycle directs your learning. A **process** rather than a set of lessons, the daily learning cycle can structure language learning at any level of proficiency, in any language. It permits you to create learning activities based on your own (self-diagnosed) language learning needs.

As mentioned in the first chapter, a complete learning cycle consists of five steps:

1. **Decide** what you want to learn for the day (or session).

2. **Prepare** materials (the content or lesson) for what you want to learn.

3. **Practice** speaking and listening, with the help of a native speaker (mentor), with a view to using your lesson in real life.

4. **Communicate** your message by speaking to native speakers outside the classroom.

5. **Evaluate** your real life experience, modify your materials and practice as needed.

You then begin the process anew—either the same day or later, depending on available time.

We will discuss each step in the pages that follow.

STEP 1: DECIDE

Traditional language teachers plan for you. The teacher tells you what to do. You listen. She directs you through the day's lesson. You respond by concentrating on performing the day's tasks in the manner prescribed by the teacher.

As a self-directed learner, you face a more difficult task. You must provide the direction and leadership formerly provided by your teacher. It is a task for which traditional instruction has left you ill-prepared.

"So," you ask, "How **do** I decide? I don't know the language. How can I possibly know what I should learn next?"

Your new decision-making responsibility is difficult. It requires thought, self-analysis, patience. Try the following.

Take time to reflect. Find a comfortable spot: the base of a banyan tree, a rocking chair, a hammock, or a rocky perch by the sea. Sit and relax. For awhile, don't worry about **doing** anything. Prepare yourself for reflection.

Define the language skills necessary for survival needs. Think about your immediate needs in living abroad: buying things, finding directions, asking questions, managing a simple conversation, getting transportation, ordering a meal. If your language skills don't permit you to perform the everyday activities you need just to get along, you have identified your initial language learning needs.

Define the language skills needed in your daily routine. Identify your most frequent activities: working, going to school, communicating with local officials, whatever. What topics do you discuss during these daily activities? What situations arise for which you need further language skill? Picture yourself in a common situation. What do you need to know how to say? What must you learn to respond to?

Define the language skills needed to expand your activities. Think about what you would like to do but feel uncomfortable doing now. Are activities off-limits to you because of limited experience, skills, or language ability? Do you want to go to particular places on your own? Attend some special event? Meet certain people? What language skills would help you fulfill those desires?

Define the language skills needed to talk about new topics. Ponder what you have seen, heard, felt since you arrived. What do you want to know that puzzles, intrigues, interests, fascinates, or upsets you? What information do you seek? What questions lie unanswered?

Define the language skills needed to enjoy life more fully. Think about yourself as a whole person, someone of many interests, moods, needs. Are you shortchanged by your limited language? What language skills will help you experience this society more fully?

Review carefully the procedures suggested in this book. Chapter 3 offers a set of language learning goals cast into a learner's checklist. Chapter 5 provides detailed lesson plans with specific words and phrases. Chapter 6 provides twelve mini-lessons and suggests dozens of practical topics, concepts, and words. Review the suggestions in these chapters. Compare them with the needs you have identified.

These suggestions address broad learning areas. From them you can develop lessons enough for months of language practice. For instance, the simple task of eating out is grist for a number of daily follow-up lessons to learn appropriate words, structures, and discussion skills for different meals—breakfast, lunch, dinner, afternoon tea, morning *merienda*, evening coffee or nightcap; for different foods and foods prepared in different ways; for asking how foods are prepared; for requesting another glass of this or an extra portion of that; for conversations in different settings. Your luncheon chat with the person on the next stool will be different from what you will say when dining with a friend at some snazzy five-star restaurant. And, though the general topics above seem to flow from basic to more complex language skills, don't assume you must exhaust one category before moving to the next. Select topics that stem from your needs, rather than from your assumptions about which structures might be difficult or easy.

In summary, your daily learning cycle begins with a specific, manageable topic for the day. That's easier said than done, but by the time you have worked your way through this book, the task will no longer seem impossible.

But wait! Before you set up your lesson, let us offer an admonition: don't let reflection be a one-time experience. Begin each day's learning with a brief planning period. Set aside time daily to think about your immediate language needs. Then decide the specific materials you will work on for the day. Time for reflection will reward you with learning that meets actual, practical needs.

With that in mind, let's run through an example of the process before we move on to step 2:

> **The Scene:** You have newly arrived in-country, settled in, and want to begin formal language study. Unfortunately, your training did not include the local language. You are starting at ground zero.
>
> **Your Thoughts:** You don't know where to begin. You have a one-word vocabulary in Pijin, the language everyone speaks here. People seem to greet each other with *mo-ne!*— probably short for "good morning." Learn something that tells people you are new here, you don't speak their language, but want to learn it.
>
> **Commentary:** OK, the task is clear. You have something specific to learn. It's short and practical. It meets an immediate need. It's not a list of words, or grammar points, or verb forms. It's something you want to learn to say to people. Let's go with it.

Step 1 is complete. You will discover how to turn this into a real Pijin conversation in step 2.

STEP 2: PREPARE

Step 2 is an easy task: create a conversation that expresses your idea in locally used language. Simple enough?

"But," you say, "that's what I'm trying to learn; how do you expect me to do it before I learn it?"

By yourself, you won't. Your mentor is the key. Because the mentor is so important to this step and to those which follow, we will devote considerable discussion to the mentor concept in chapter 4.

For right now, think for a moment about what you are after here. In general, you want to take your thoughts about what you want to learn and turn them into real words in the target language. You want your conversation to be phrased in terms that people use in everyday speech.

Distinguish between *proper* and *common* usage. A simple question in English, "Where are you going, Bob?" is frequently stated as "Where ya goin'?" You want common usage, language people normally speak in situations in which you are likely to find yourself.

You also want your conversation to be phrased in the locally appropriate framework. Distinguish between *formal* and *informal* speech. As an example, in formally addressing a teacher, you might say, "Good morning, Mr. Johnston. How are you today?" If he were a friend or colleague, you might greet him more informally: "Mornin', Bob, how ya doin'?" or "How's it goin'?" Appropriate speech varies. You speak one way with your friends, differently when you address your professors. Likewise, different cultures, contexts, and personal relationships require different words, topics, sentence structures. It might be that in the target language someone of your position simply would not address Mr. Johnston informally. Perhaps no local equivalent exists for "good morning." Maybe greetings require other words, or gestures rather than words. Perhaps they are handled in some other way.

You want expressions appropriate to the context, not translations of how you speak at home.

You must convey to your mentor a **sense** of what you want to say. Help your mentor visualize those images dancing in your mind, rather than translate specific words. You set the stage, convey a sense of the emotion and meaning you wish to express. Half your task is to listen, to make sure your mentor provides appropriate messages rather than direct translation.

Again, more easily said than done! Look for indirect cues that your mentor knows your passage should not be translated directly: hesitation, eye and body movement, verbal agreement followed by subtle, but contradictory, suggestions. As you work with an individual and as you become more attuned to the society's cultural cues, you will recognize messages being sent you. If your mentor is bilingual, have him translate his translation back into English—it should sound different from the way you said it the first time.

In summary, the task is to convey your proposed messages into appropriate target language. That means turning your mentor's words into something specific and probably tangible, most likely either written sentences or a tape recording. Once that has been completed—take your time, it may take fifteen minutes or an hour—you will have finished step 2. Before we move on, let's update our example:

> **The Scene:** With a simple introductory statement in mind, you have, with the help of a mentor, converted an idea into target language conversation.

> **Your Actions:** You convey your intent to your mentor. You want to approach people—both friends and strangers—tell them you are new here, that you don't speak their language yet, but that you want to learn it. Then you want to end the conversation by saying that's all you know and depart with some appropriate goodbye.

> Use gestures. With your mentor try to visualize a situation rather than give specific English sentences to translate.

> **The Result:** Together you come up with the following: *Mi gogo ahed fo lanim Pijin blong Solomone, ia. Hem nao evri samting wea mi nao save long hem. Taggio tumas fo herem toktoko blong mi, ia.* (If you are not familiar with Pijin, read it aloud word for word. See, it makes sense already!)

> **Commentary:** OK, you have something to work with. They are real sentences, not lists of vocabulary words, not grammar points, not verb forms, not rules. But look! As you master this passage, you will learn a beginning vocabulary. You will learn some basic sentence structures. You will learn a sound commonly used to end sentences. You will know how to close a conversation and thank someone. In the process you will learn how sentences flow—where to pause, where to accent, where your voice should rise and fall—and you will practice pronunciation. All of this without thinking about anything more than the first message you want to convey!

STEP 3: PRACTICE

You seek oral fluency. You want to talk to people and respond when they talk to you. To do that, you have to listen and speak; speak and listen. Then, when you tire of speaking, speak again.

Oral practice is difficult. Our educational system emphasizes reading and writing as early as those first school days when our chief concern is how to get across the street safely. Try something radical: practice each new passage or conversation orally. Don't read! Don't even glance at the written word. You will resist the idea. But try it for these reasons:

- You need to master language flow and pronunciation as well as individual words.

Reading distorts your image of the target language. Because you read with English-speaking eyes, reading encourages you to pronounce as you would pronounce English words. This builds incorrect pronunciation and phrasing habits.

- You need to develop listening skills.

Teaching your tongue to twist unnaturally around new sounds is only half the task. You also need to train your hearing to pick out the messages in those rapid bursts of syllables people shoot at you. Oral practice fosters listening as well as speaking.

- You need to learn conversation techniques.

Conversation is more than words spoken and words heard. People emphasize, modify, negate their words with eye and body movements and gestures. Oral practice frees your eyes to look for the visual cues essential to communication.

Now, let's run through a sample practice session.

1. **Practice listening: have your mentor recite the passage.**

First, ask your mentor to recite the passage at normal conversation speed. Just listen for the flow of the passage, for its music, for pauses, for tones as they rise and fall. Suspend your natural desire to understand every word you hear. Relax; it doesn't matter that you don't understand the words—this is a listening exercise. Don't panic; you don't have to reproduce what you hear yet. Just listen to the passage enough times to develop a feel for how it sounds, to sense the rhythm. How many times? You may need three or four times; or you may need ten or fifteen times. Listen until the passage sounds familiar, comfortable.

Then, listen to each sentence a few times at normal speed, again for flow, pronunciation, feeling.

Next, ask your mentor to recite each sentence at a slower speed. Listen for words and sounds. Try to pick out individual words which may be repeated in different sentences, or different locations in the same sentence. Again, don't worry about speaking. Relax and listen. See if you can distinguish sounds. Listen until the passage becomes less a blur and more a combination of different sounds, until you hear clear sentences, individual words.

And again, don't worry about meaning. You already know what it means (after all, the passage was your idea). The exact meaning of individual words will come with practice.

2. **Practice pronunciation and retention: have your mentor drill you on each sentence.**

At first, even a simple sentence will twist your tongue. Ask your mentor to guide you through each sentence in smaller bites. Have him (or her) take one sentence at a time and break it into natural pieces. Practice each, building on success until you have mastered each full sentence. Go at it a sentence at a time, building **backwards** from the end of each sentence. (This helps you repeat the entire sentence more easily as well as produce it in a more natural way.) Remember that your aim is to say the passage fluently and easily from memory. This will require you to repeat the passage many times.

Here the goal is to produce sentences in spoken form. Again, don't worry about understanding each word, each sound. Concentrate on repetition. Resist the urge to have your mentor define words. One of the sublime joys of language learning comes with those sudden flashes when you realize what a word means from its context. Remind yourself that you do know the meaning of the whole passage. Be patient and let individual word meanings come to you on their own.

Your practice will go something like this, with your mentor speaking first and you repeating:

Mentor:...*blong Solomone, ia*	**L:**...*blong Solomone, ia.*
M:...*blong Solomone, ia.*	**L:**...*blong Solomone, ia.*
M:...*blong Solomone, ia.*	**L:**...*blong Solomone, ia.*
M: *(Gestures for repetition)*	**L:**...*blong Solomone, ia.*
M:...*fo lanim Pijin...*	**L:**...*fo lanim Pijin...*
M:...*fo lanim Pijin...*	**L:**...*fo lanim Pijin...*
M:...*fo lanim Pijin...*	**L:**...*fo lanim Pijin...*
M: *(Gestures for repetition)*	**L:**...*fo lanim Pijin...*

M:...*fo lanim Pijin blong Solomone, ia.*
        L:...*fo lanim Pijin blong Solomone, ia.*
M:...*fo lanim Pijin blong Solomone, ia.*
        L:...*fo lanim Pijin blong Solomone, ia.*
M:...*fo lanim Pijin blong Solomone, ia.*
        L:...*fo lanim Pijin blong Solomone, ia.*
M: *(Gestures for repetition)*
        L:...*fo lanim Pijin blong Solomone, ia.*

M: Mi nao gogo ahed...:   *L: Mi nao gogo ahed...*
M: Mi nao gogo ahed...:   *L: Mi nao gogo ahed...*
M: Mi nao gogo ahed...:   *L: Mi nao gogo ahed...*
M: (Gestures for repetition)   *L: Mi nao gogo ahed...*

M: Mi nao gogo ahed fo lanim Pijin blong Solomone, ia.
    L: Mi nao gogo ahed fo lanim Pijin blong Solomone, ia.
M: Mi nao gogo ahed fo lanim Pijin blong Solomone, ia.
    L: Mi nao gogo ahed fo lanim Pijin blong Solomone, ia.
M: Mi nao gogo ahed fo lanim Pijin blong Solomone, ia.
    L: Mi nao gogo ahed fo lanim Pijin blong Solomone, ia.
M: (Gestures for repetition)
    L: Mi nao gogo ahed fo lanim Pijin blong Solomone, ia.

It's a simple technique, but effective. It enables you to concentrate on smaller, more manageable pieces of the sentence while getting a feel for its flow and tone.

Build gradually this way, piece by piece until you master each sentence. Practice the first two sentences together. Add the third. Build up to the entire passage. Don't be discouraged if you stumble on some of the earlier sentences and phrases as you approach the end of the entire passage. That's normal. Run through them again, and again, and again....

3. **Role-play: act out the passage with your mentor.**

Once you can repeat the passage freely, act it out. Let your mentor (and your partners if you are learning with others) be the old man at the wharf, the group in the market, or whomever the sentence is aimed at. Practice walking up to them. Work on your approach, your smile, your stance, your gestures, as well as the words of the passage.

Drilling helps you memorize the passage. Roleplaying teaches you to deliver it to other people, smoothly, fluently, naturally.

4. **Modify your passage: revise it if it doesn't sound authentic.**

As you practice your passage, have your mentor respond as in natural conversation with comments you might hear from strangers: "Oh, how interesting!" "You must be Peace Corps; other foreigners don't speak Pijin!" "It's nice to meet you, sir!" "Hey, that's good, man!" "What did he say? I couldn't understand him!"

Will a particular response require you to change one of your original sentences? It might. Or it might require another sentence. Chances are, your practice will point out to both you and your mentor needed changes in your passage. If it does, modify your passage, relearn it, practice some more. And don't fret. Changes don't mean your earlier practice was for naught; changes mean you have expanded beyond your original intent.

5. **Drill for structure: have your mentor teach you variations.**

Each memorized passage not only teaches you vocabulary and messages for a particular situation, but provides basic sentence structures for a variety of situations. Each sentence in your dialogue becomes a pattern you can use in a new drill; your dialogue thus spawns a wealth of discussion beyond the situation for which it was developed. As you gain vocabulary and fluency, you will want to add other drills to vary your practice and develop different skills.

Learn the basic pattern drills below. They will help you master your passage, as well as expand its usefulness. As you gain skill, you can make your drills more complicated.

• **Substitution.** This drill reinforces a particular (common) sentence pattern by substituting different words in that pattern. In doing this, you gain mastery over that structure at the same time as you expand the volume of what you are able to say. Let's use as an example an English translation of a sentence from our initial Pijin passage, "I am learning Pijin." (Practice in the target language, not English.)

In this sentence, we might begin by substituting words for "learning," expanding our use of action words. To do this, your mentor would say, "I am learning Pijin." You would repeat, "I am learning Pijin." He would then give you a one-word cue, such as "studying," and you would say, "I am studying Pijin." After the initial sentence in this drill, your mentor says only the appropriate word (in Pijin), and you repeat the **entire sentence**, inserting the new word in the proper place. This exercise helps drive home the sentence pattern, but it also builds vocabulary. The drill below is good for starters. Remember, all drilling is in the target language.

M: I am **learning** Pijin.	L: I am **learning** Pijin.
M: **studying**	L: I am **studying** Pijin.
M: **speaking**	L: I am **speaking** Pijin.
M: **writing**	L: I am **writing** Pijin.
M: **listening to**	L: I am **listening to** Pijin.
M: **reading**	L: I am **reading** Pijin.
	etc.

Be alert to substitutions which change other words in the sentence. These are more complicated and should be practiced in the same way—but only after you have gained control of the simpler substitutions. These idiosyncracies will vary from language to language. An example in

English would involve changing the subject pronoun, which causes changes in the verb:

M: *I am* learning Pijin.	L: *I am* learning Pijin.
M: *He*	L: *He is* learning Pijin.
M: *They*	L: *They are* learning Pijin.
M: *We*	L: *We are* learning Pijin.
	etc.

As you improve, make the drill more challenging by having your mentor vary the slot or position of the substitution, requiring you to place the new word in a different position. For example:

M: I am learning Pijin.	L: I am learning Pijin.
M: **cricket**	L: I am learning **cricket**.
M: **playing**	L: I am **playing** cricket.
M: **He**	L: **He is** playing cricket.
	etc.

• **Expansion.** In this drill, you build on your basic sentence pattern to make it more complicated by having your mentor add a new idea. An example, again in English:

M: I am learning Pijin.	L: I am learning Pijin.
M: **from my friend**	L: I am learning Pijin **from my friend.**
M: I am reading Pijin.	L: I am reading Pijin.
M: **from a book**	L: I am reading Pijin **from a book.**
M: He is playing football.	L: He is playing football.
M: **with the boys**	L: He is playing football **with the boys.**
	etc.

This drill strengthens your grasp of the basic sentence and expands the sentence for use in other situations. Once your mentor catches on to the idea, this drill can be creative and fun for both of you.

• **Transformation.** This drill requires you to rework the basic sentence based on your understanding of the language. The most basic transformations include negative, tense or time changes, questions, active/passive voice. To learn negative statements, for instance, you

PRODUCTIVE PRACTICE:
Hints for an Effective Study Session

What makes a practice session productive? Hard work? Of course! Also, keep these tricks in mind; they should help you study effectively.

Practice orally.   Listen to your mentor talk. Speak, and then speak some more. Neither read nor write during the session.

Practice constantly.   Utilize your practice time fully. Avoid digressions. As your mentor speaks, mouth the words silently. Concentrate on learning, not simply completing the exercises.

Drill thoroughly.   The drills in the text are *examples* of possible variations. Create as many variations as you can handle. Practice your drills until you can produce them fluently. You want to become fluent, not merely complete each drill.

Avoid English.   Urge your mentor to speak in the target language. To communicate ideas you can't otherwise express, use circumlocutions, gestures, sign language, but try to *speak* in the target language whenever possible. Using English promotes translation, if only inside your head. That delays your thinking in the target language and postpones fluency.

Have faith.   Your mentor speaks in certain ways because that's the way people say things. Don't ask *why*. Worry about production rather than explanation. Accept on faith that understanding will come. It will. If you must question, ask *when*. Your mentor can more easily tell you when to use a certain construction than why it is used.

Intuit meaning.   You understand your overall passage because you developed it. Learn individual words from context; don't ask for translations. Intuit their meaning, then try them in new sentences. Ask your mentor to develop sentences using the words you don't understand. Develop images of word meanings rather than definitions in translation.

Intuit grammar.   Your mentor provides patterns and practice. Don't let him become a grammar instructor. To repeat, he explains *what* or *when*, not *why*. Understand patterns (grammar) by intuiting them. Don't ask for them to be explained. Grammatical explanations divert you.

Record your passage.   If you have a cassette recorder, tape your mentor speaking (not reading) your passage. Practice by yourself later. First, record the full passage at normal speed, followed by a pause long enough for you to think about the whole passage. Then record each sentence with a pause long enough for you to repeat it twice, and then each sentence at a slower speed. Next, record the full passage with a long enough pause at the end to repeat the entire passage, and finally, record the full passage again at normal speed.

Rest your brain and mouth.   Periodically relax. Drink a cup of coffee or a glass of guava juice. Play ping pong. But take your break in the target language—change subjects, not the language. Chat about the snack, weather, current events, or just listen. Switching to English provides more rest but disrupts your thought patterns and eliminates the possibility that learning will continue in the informality of break time.

might begin with your basic pattern and have your mentor give you a negative cue (either a word or a negative gesture):

M: He is learning Pijin.	*L: He is learning Pijin.*
*M: **not***	*L: He is **not** learning Pijin.*
M: I am playing ball.	*L: I am playing ball.*
M: (negative gesture)	*L: I am **not** playing ball.*
	etc.

Another transformation moves from present time to past time, as in the following:

M: He is studying Pijin.	*L: He is studying Pijin.*
*M: **Yesterday***	*L: He **was** studying Pijin **yesterday**.*
*M: **Now***	*L: He **is** studying Pijin **now**.*
*M: **Last week***	*L: He **was** studying Pijin **last week**.*
	etc.

This drill adapts your basic sentence into other structures as you learn to manipulate sentence forms.

• **Combination.**   These are drills which require you to combine more simple pattern changes. An English example:

M: I am learning to speak Pijin.	*L: I am learning to speak Pijin.*
*M: **cook rice***	*L: I am learning to **cook rice**.*
*M: **He***	*L: **He is** learning to cook rice.*
*M: **They***	*L: **They are** learning to cook rice.*
*M: **Yesterday***	*L: They **were learning** to cook rice **yesterday**.*
*M: **We***	*L: **We** were learning to cook rice yesterday.*
M: (negative gesture)	*L: We **weren't** learning to cook rice yesterday.*
	etc.

The combination drill provides extensive practice in manipulating sentences. It offers an infinite variety of patterns, vocabulary, and sentence structures.

One caution when using any of these drills: you will sometimes end up with sentences that don't make sense in the target language or just wouldn't be said. Caution your mentor not to let you practice awkward or unacceptable sentences. An example in English might be: "He was learning Pijin yesterday." Learning takes place over a long period of time and isn't accomplished today or tomorrow. "Studying" would be much more appropriate.

The above are simple, beginning-level drills. Once you have the basics down, go on to more complicated drills which move beyond simple repetition and substitution. Two examples follow:

• **Vocabulary Flexibility Drill.** This drill helps you to develop fuller meaning of particular words in your vocabulary.

Once you have moved beyond basic sentence patterns, you will find that the same word crops up in different contexts. This drill helps establish the fuller meaning of the word (and provides a basic structure to define other words). Here is an example in which you identify a new word, then expand your understanding of its meaning through further definition. (The sentence used would, of course, vary with the context.)

> **Learner** *(pointing at an object): What is that?*
> **Mentor:** *It's a* mocajete!
> **L:** *Mocajete? Did you say mocajete?*
> **M:** *Yes, this is a mocajete.*
> **L:** *I see, it's a mocajete. What do you do with a mocajete?*
> **M:** *We grind chile with it.*
> **L:** *You do? You use a mocajete to grind chile?*
> **M:** *We sure do.*
> **L:** *Do you use a mocajete to grind other things? Corn?*
> **M:** *Yes, we also grind corn with a mocajete.*
> **L:** *I see, you grind chile and corn with a mocajete.*

In this drill, you build on information provided by the mentor, paraphrasing, rather than repeating the exact words. But, by using the target word frequently, you more quickly master its use. This dialog could continue as you talk about other uses of a mocajete, the material from which a mocajete is made, other tools, food preparation, etc.

• **Communicative Appropriateness Exercise.** This exercise helps you build communicative competence by practicing and learning acceptable responses to a situation. You will learn a great deal about communication and culture through this discussion and practice. Try building exercises around other situations: making an invitation, accepting a compliment, greetings with various ages and positions, partings, excuses, accepting an invitation, clarifying misunderstandings, telephone etiquette, etc. Here is an example of refusing an invitation:

> **Mentor:** *Can you go to the movie with us?*
> **Learner:** *I'm sorry, I can't; I have to study.*
> *No, I can't; I have work to do.*
> *I wish I could, but I'm not feeling well.*
> *Of course; just a second while I change.*
> *Thank you for asking; I would be delighted.*
> *etc.*

For this exercise, you first develop a set of likely responses, then, if necessary, use a simple pattern drill to learn each response. With your mentor, agree on a common set of cues—either verbal cues (e.g., "I have to work.") or visual cues (nodding or shaking of head for yes and no; some hand signal for "study," "work," "being ill," etc.). Your mentor provides the cue, and you respond appropriately.

The exercise provides opportunity to develop greater flexibility in responding to questions than simple pattern drills and helps you develop communicative competence.

An endless variety of drills and exercises can be created to practice particular responses, phrasing, vocabulary building, pronunciation, etc. In general, drills help build fluent, smooth patterns en route to using those patterns in normal conversation. Creativity in drilling comes in developing the appropriate structures. The actual drilling can be tiresome and repetitious. Remember, drilling isn't an end in itself; it's a method of practice.

Let's summarize your work in step 3. Your idea has become a spoken message. Step 3 has been a formal class (with structure, drills, formal practice), but it seemed informal. It prepared you to speak with people in the community. Before you head out in step 4, let's recap our example.

> **The Scene:** You completed "formal" practice with your mentor. You are ready now to try your memorized passage on people you don't know.

> **Your Actions:** You learned your conversation piece by piece, sentence by sentence. You listened to tone, pronunciation, flow. You practiced speaking, building from sentence fragments to whole sentences, and from sentences to a whole paragraph. You roleplayed the passage with your mentor.

> **The Result:** Your first passage was too limiting. It didn't prepare you for a response. You revised it:

> **Learner:** *Mi gogo ahed fo lanim Pijin blong Solomone, ia.*

Hem nao evri samting wea mi nao save long hem. Taggio tumas fo herem toktoko blong mi, ia.

    Respondent: *Hem nao. Iu save tumas, man!*

    Learner: *Taggio tumas, fren. Mi bae go nao, ia.*

You modified your original passage to make it fit at least one anticipated response. You added a conversation closure. The passage is a bit longer, but you can say it all, nearly without pause. Your pronunciation seems understandable. You are a bit hesitant, but confident that you are ready to go out and try it.

    Commentary: Your practice hasn't ended yet. You have merely prepared for real-life practice, this time in an uncontrolled setting. You learned to manipulate your basic sentences. You learned some words. You have a basic format and an idea of some likely variations—a learned and modified passage—that will serve as springboards for community-based learning. You also have an ice-breaker to open conversations with people you don't know. As you move on to step 4, keep in mind that the product of your intense effort thus far will undergo further modification from the range of native speakers you are about to meet.

STEP 4: COMMUNICATE

Armed with your short passage and a bit of chutzpa, you are ready to apply your new knowledge to real life.

If you like to meander through village streets, your task is an easy one. An unhurried gait, an observant eye, and an occasional pause to gaze at the blossoming frangipani create an excellent mien for chatting unhurriedly with a village elder, an open-air shopkeeper, or a loitering youth. In such a setting, a casual greeting fits the customary pattern of life. Pause or smile or otherwise show interest, and, when people respond, speak to them.

Pijin speakers have an apt term for such strolling: *wokabaot.* You stop when you feel like it; you continue when the mood strikes. You are not out to accomplish anything; you simply walk about. The wokabaot is a natural venue to meet people, especially people you don't know.

City life can be more difficult. The thundering rush-hour crowd in the Tokyo subway isn't receptive to your *gaijin* Japanese. Nor will you elicit much response from a snake charmer in the bedlam of the Marrakech public market. But busy cities have their byways and neighborhoods, their parks and cafes. In the city, you can go to work, school, or shopping by the same route daily. You will begin to recognize individual faces; people will begin to recognize you. Try your passage on those people who smile, or nod, or show some sign of recognition. As you gain fluency and as people get to know you, they become welcome guideposts along your way.

Each of us approaches people in a different way. A style that works for some is ineffective for others. We must reach out and meet new people in a style comfortable for us. While there is no magic formula, some simple suggestions can help.

Build on your mentor's natural ties to the community. Initially, go wokabaot with your mentor, not as an interpreter, but to introduce you to his friends, people he knows will be receptive and helpful.

Ask your mentor to make note of your major mistakes, of cultural messages, and customs exhibited on the wokabaot. You can discuss them *after* you have returned from the wokabaot (immediate correction is too likely to disrupt your thinking, and inhibit you.) Don't let your mentor talk *for* you—after all, he doesn't need the practice.

Start with the places most familiar to you. Begin in your own neighborhood. Children, the people next door, the woman across the street—people who see you often and recognize you as a neighborhood resident—are likely candidates for conversation. Begin with your neighbors; become a member of the neighborhood in which you live.

Haunt locales not frequented by fellow expatriates. Speaking to strolling lovers on the Champs Elysees isn't the best place to brush up on your French. Too many tourists, too many Americans have preceded you (and your targeted couple may have thoughts on their minds other than your language development). Find neighborhoods where residents carry out their daily routine in the target language.

Choose with care the timing of your language outings. People rushing to work aren't inclined to stop and chat, even if they know you. Nor can the restaurateur visit while the midday crowd descends on his cafe. Others may be more receptive: afternoon browsers, Sunday strollers, vendors during their slow hours. Your visits must add something to their day—even if only a moment of respite or a chuckle—as well as bolster your speaking skills.

Be sensitive to competing demands upon those whom you ask for help.

Use an approach which seems natural and comfortable to you. You want to develop relationships with people as you learn their language and culture. To relate to people as people, your actions must fit your personality. If you are naturally gregarious, no problem; you know what to do. If you are shy, more given to business transactions than friendly chitchat with strangers, build on that habit. Go first to shops, seek advice, look for particular items, buy something as a way to initiate conversation. Let your own habits help you establish conversations and relationships.

Step 4 of the learning cycle nudges you outward. Go into the community, find people, talk to them. Use your prepared passage as a conversation opener. Exactly how you approach people and engage them in conversation will flow from your own personal interaction style and skill.

No matter what your tack, however, move from classroom to community. Reach out, engage everyday people in conversation. You will learn from people who speak differently from one another, who use different gestures, accents, ways to express the same ideas. The first three steps of the learning cycle help you prepare for your in situ education. Immersion in the language environment nurtures your real learning.

Your education doesn't end when you go into the community, however. You complete the learning cycle when you step back, analyze your experience, and learn from it. You will do that in step 5. First, let's summarize what you have done here.

> **The scene:** You strolled down the street, past the wharf, and ended up in the marketplace.
>
> **Your actions:** You tried your passage on an old man seated near the wharf and on a group of teenagers. In the market you bought bananas and a papaya and spoke to a vendor and two other shoppers.
>
> **The result:** The old man didn't understand you. You repeated your passage. He mumbled something, then wandered off. The teenagers laughed; one shouted something. One youngster repeated the passage twice, then had you say it again—much to the amusement of his friends. At the market, several people chuckled. They seemed surprised that you wanted to learn their language. Two listened and smiled, and one repeated the entire passage, correcting your pronunciation.
>
> **Commentary:** OK, you've got the drift. You went out. You engaged people in conversation. You spoke; you listened. It didn't always work—the old man obviously didn't understand you, so something is wrong. But the others did, and two actually helped you a bit. Your passage worked, at least in part.

STEP 5: EVALUATE

Memorized passages won't prepare you for every possibility. At best, by focusing attention on given topics and specific structures, they give you confidence. They provide a model. You modify them as you join more fully in natural conversation.

No matter how well you plan, you will find that you need variations—not because you've done anything wrong; it's just a fact of life. As you think about your own English language usage, you will understand why.

Native speakers express the same ideas in different words. At the simplest level, think of our many English greetings: "Good morning," "Howdy," "How are you?" "How're things goin'?" "What's up?" etc. They mean basically the same thing, but think how confusing they could be if you knew only one, "Good morning," and someone greeted you with "What's up?" That happens frequently as you learn a second language.

Native speakers use different emphases to change the meaning of their words. "**I'm** going to the wharf" tells something I am going to do. But, "I'm going to the **wharf**" emphasizes the location. If you listen for one emphasis and the speaker uses another, you may easily misunderstand.

Native speakers sometimes hear meaning different from the words that were spoken. Listen carefully to friends talking. People often talk past one another; they respond to their own thoughts rather than the words spoken by their fellow conversationalists.

Native speakers don't always speak clearly or correctly. People slur words, mumble them, omit them, mispronounce them, use incorrect grammar, and even throw in wrong words from time to time. Native speakers understand each other because they can grasp the context of the conversation, even if some of the individual words are unintelligible or wrong. Additionally, native speakers sometimes simply misunderstand each other because they speak imprecisely.

Native speakers interrupt or change direction in midstream. magine approaching a group of teenagers. You get halfway through your passage when one youth blurts out, "*Oh fren, mi laekim tumas calico blong iu!*" ("Hey, I really like your shirt!") It has no relation to your prepared passage; as a new learner you are unprepared to respond. It happens frequently, among native speakers as well as cross-culturally.

Native speakers respond to what they think people say, rather than to what people actually say. Sometimes we think ahead as others talk, anticipate what they are going to say, then answer incorrectly because we weren't listening closely to their exact words. Additionally, when we talk to foreigners (and they talk to us) we sometimes presume subconsciously that we won't understand them. Then, when they speak, even if in impeccable English, we prove ourselves right.

In short, perfect communication based on a learned passage is unlikely—not because of something you did or didn't do, but because of the nature of how people communicate with one another. You compensate, not by giving up in despair, but by viewing community involvement as an opportunity to parry and thrust in response to unanticipated situations.

Evaluation begins during the wokabaot. Your mentor interprets the unanticipated, points out variations that require changes in your passage, explains responses you missed.

Once you start venturing out on your own, concentrate on observing as well as speaking and listening. Record mentally the variations you encounter and the responses that didn't meet your expectations. Then, discuss your experiences with your mentor and prepare for similar situations in the future.

In general, evaluation and analysis is a two-step process. First, identify and record your experiences during your wokabaot. You don't need to carry a video camera, Super-8, or cassette recorder to record your experiences for analysis. Rather, pause occasionally to jot down in a pocket-sized notebook the main events, the threads of conversation, the gestures, your feeling about what happened, what worked and what didn't. Ask yourself, "What variations in words, sounds, gestures did I notice?" "How did people respond to what I said?" "What did people say that I couldn't respond to?" Record enough so that you can verbally recreate each situation for your mentor.

Second, discuss and analyze your experiences. Describe to your mentor reactions and responses you got to your prepared passage. Ask yourself, "Should some sentences be revised? Some phrases or words added or deleted? Which ones? How?" Then, revise your original passage.

Beyond your review of the initial passage, your evaluation will extend to planning for broader participation in similar situations in the future. Ask yourself, "What things happened or were said that suggest additional preparation? Did I see or hear things I want to discuss further? Are there feelings I need to know how to express? Did my experience raise questions about the culture, about people's actions?"

From such questions come ideas for revising the initial passage, elaborating on it, or creating new passages. The cycle begins anew as you analyze, revise, and practice the revisions. Let's take a final look at our first wokabaot.

> **The Scene:** With your mentor, you have completed your wokabaot past the wharf and to the marketplace. You are back at your original meeting place.

> **Your Actions:** You analyze what happened—meeting the old man; your brief encounter with the youths, one of whom shouted something you didn't understand; and the discussion in the marketplace with the vendor and two customers. You recreate each scene, recall as best you can who said what. You try to figure out what would have made each situation go more smoothly.

> **The Result:** You realize that your initial sentence was too businesslike. So, you add an introductory greeting. *Halo fren, waswe!* would be appropriate, your mentor explains. You add a couple of markers—a simple *hem nao, ia* to express agreement, and a *taggio tumas* to express appreciation. Your mentor develops a drill using *mi laekim …* so you can practice the taggio tumas phrase. You learn to respond to it, and to use it to compliment others.

> Finally, you learn a cultural lesson—the old man, a member of a mountain tribe, is visiting in the city. His language is Kwaio; he doesn't speak Pijin at all. He wouldn't have responded to your Pijin no matter how clearly you spoke it.

> **Commentary:** Analysis and evaluation teach lessons based directly on personal experience. They expand your understanding beyond your capacity to observe culturally new events. Further, they give you specific sounding boards from which to develop follow-up planning, practice, and community study.

Three

Goals:
Benchmarks for Evaluation

The measure of success in language learning is the ability to use the language. We are successful if we can talk to and understand native speakers in normal conversation.

We could set more demanding goals, of course, such as being able to discuss the great literature of the language or negotiate international agreements, but it is better if goals reflect what we honestly hope and expect to accomplish.

Goals determine the plan of action and provide the measure by which to evaluate language learning progress. Whatever our goals, we want to express them in terms that enable us to determine if in fact we have met them. The courses taken, textbooks and assignments completed, drills repeated, or hours studied do not measure achievement. Such activities are only means by which we strive to meet our goals.

This chapter provides a framework for effective goal setting, a continuing process that uses goals as tools for learning.

GOAL SETTING

A goal setting framework is essential to the self-directed learner. **You** must decide what activities to undertake. The strength of your daily learning cycle rests upon your ability to develop tasks appropriate to goals that you determine are important. You are on your own. No teacher will define what you need to learn, direct your study, or test your progress.

Goals help direct your learning. They provide a framework to help you choose from many possibilities that which is most important to you. Goals should serve you. They should not become merely an added assignment. Useful goals will

1. describe what is expected of you.

Effective goals delineate clearly and precisely expected performance. The more precise the definition, the more easily you can determine appropriate learning activities and decide if you have successfully met your goals. The goal may be simple—"(I will) order a meal from a restaurant menu"—but even a simple goal tells you what you have to do to meet it.

2. constitute realistic, yet challenging expectations.

Effective goals are achievable. They take into account your abilities, available time, competing demands. If you examine your goals and conclude, "It's useless; I'll never meet those goals!" the goals are unrealistic. Revise them. On the other hand, goals must challenge you, push you to achieve. You can write goals that you can reach without effort. Don't bother. Use goals to help you learn, not to collect gold stars.

3. focus on a process rather than a one-shot assignment.

Effective goal setting, like the learning cycle, is continuous. Don't sit down, write goals, and then file them away. Goals should be reevaluated constantly to make sure they are appropriate.

Achieving your goals isn't a test of will power. Don't write them down once and expect them to keep you forever on task. Using the learning cycle, you set goals, undertake specific learning activities, then evaluate both according to whether you've met the goals and **whether the goals themselves were appropriate**. If the goals are unrealistic, change them.

4. serve both as a guide and as a means to evaluate your achievement.

Effective goals specify targets you hope to reach. Additionally, they state the standards by which you judge your performance to determine if your efforts have succeeded. The goal, "I will act as an interpreter at a professional meeting or function," not only hints at the kind of practice needed to achieve this level of language ability, it also sets a standard by which you judge your achievement—can you or can you not interpret at a professional meeting?

The Language Learner's Proficiency Scale, included at the end of this chapter, describes ability levels that you can use to estimate your language skill. Compare this scale to your own needs. Define the abilities you want in your new language. Then ask yourself the questions below. Your goals will emerge naturally from the exercise.

1. What abilities do I need to carry out my normal routine?

Will you be called upon to translate for others? Merely to respond to simple requests in the target language? To argue cogently in your new language at professional meetings? To discuss current events with coworkers or neighbors? To buy food and supplies without a hassle?

You may wish to define a minimum and an optimum level of attainment. For example, it may be imperative that you talk about work-related matters with your colleagues. This would be your minimum level of acceptable language proficiency. Work would be more enjoyable, though, if you also understood the break-time puns, jokes, and double entendres your coworkers so freely swap. This is your optimum level of attainment.

Identify the achievement level that will allow you to satisfy your needs.

2. How much time do I have to spend on language learning?

If you have settled in for two years, you will have more time for language learning than if you are overseas for the summer. If you are unfettered by full-time employment, you will have more time than if you teach full time or work on a construction site. Be realistic. You won't achieve native-speaking fluency in three months if you study only an hour a day.

Language learning isn't your only activity. You have work or schooling, commitments to family and friends, parenting, household tasks, a desire to visit historic sites or attend particular events. Sometimes those activities mesh with language learning. Sometimes they don't. Look realistically at what you do and what you want to do.

Unless you rank language mastery a high priority, you will find it difficult to consistently allocate large blocks of time to it. If you believe that other activities are more important, you shouldn't expect to reach a proficiency level as high as if language were your chief concern.

3. How important is it that I reach (x) level of ability?

Think carefully about your own needs, not the admonitions of others. You want goals which are realistic, meaningful, and feasible for you—not for your spouse, your mother-in-law, or your friends back home.

4. How much does my normal daily routine bring me in contact with native speakers?

If you teach English as a second language in an urban secondary school in Kenya, you will speak less Swahili than if you teach basic health care in a rural village. If you manage a computer team automating the ministry's data-processing system in a former British colony, you will speak more English on the job than if you supervise dockworkers in the same country. Likewise, if you live in an expatriate subdivision in Germany, travel the diplomatic circuit, spend your free time on the military base or with parents of children at the international school, you will speak more English than if your daily activities bring you into contact with native speakers.

Obviously, the more exposure you have to native-speaking situations in your normal work and living routine, the higher you can set your language learning goals.

Goal setting should be useful. Consider the above and then set goals which recognize your circumstances. Your goals should challenge you, but they should not be impossible to reach.

Keep in mind that goals needn't be writ in stone. Feel free to change, modify, or delete as you become more (or less) fluent, and as your situation, needs, and desires change.

The partner of goal setting is evaluation—not formal examinations, tests, or panel reviews, but some periodic, semiobjective review of your progress toward your goals. Use the Language Learner's Proficiency Scale in this chapter as your guide.

Goal setting and evaluation are most easily done (and are most effective) as part of your normal routine rather than as some added (and odious) task. Begin your daily learning cycle with a goal-setting exercise. End each day's lesson with a review. The following will help you integrate goal setting and evaluation into your schedule:

1. Lay out weekly goals as an overview to your daily activities.

Weekly goals provide a framework for each day's goals. They put day-by-day activities into a larger context, allow you to look beyond today to long-range needs. They help you view daily activities as a series of connected events that together move you in some desired direction.

2. Keep a journal, and use it to record your progress.

Your journal records your overseas experience. It's a wonderful memento. It is also a practical instrument to help you measure your progress. Use it to summarize your activities, record the highlights of your day or week, reflect on where you have been and where you are going. As part of journal writing, think about your language learning progress. Jot down a summary of how you believe you are doing.

3. Summarize your progress in letters to friends.

Most of us write to someone during our stay abroad. Use your letter writing as an opportunity to reflect on your language learning. Add a paragraph describing your language-learning activities. Summarize your progress. Tell your friends what you will work on next. They will be interested in your language learning—and you will have put both goals and evaluation in writing. (Keep a copy, of course.)

4. Take stock of your progress on a periodic basis.

It's easy to bog down in day-to-day living. From ground level, progress often seems agonizingly slow. Interestingly enough, the perspective gained from stepping back from time to time not only helps redirect your efforts, it also helps you see that you've made more progress than you had imagined. Look not only at where you are going, but also back to where you began.

Set aside an occasional halfday to review your weekly goals, examine your progress, and lay out general directions for the next three months.

5. Gear the review of your language learning progress to other reports you have to make.

Any reporting requires recall and reflection and thus provides a good context in which to take stock of your progress. If your employment requires reports—time sheets; weekly, monthly, or project reports—assess your language progress at the same time.

In summary, goal setting will be most effective if viewed as an integral part of your normal routine. You are busy. Don't try to add another hour to a hectic schedule; plan goal setting as part of your ongoing activities.

Writing your goals helps direct your learning and points you toward activities which make the best use of study time. The process of physically writing down your goals gives you clear direction in determining appropriate language learning activities. Written goals help your mentor (and fellow learners) assist you in developing learning activities which effectively target your goals. Further, written goals provide a record which allows you to review your progress more precisely.

Let's work through the process of goal setting with an example.

1. Define the general goal as precisely as possible.

Let's use the goal, "to develop my ability to speak on the telephone." Phone conversation commonly presents a problem: thoughts easily expressed in person seem difficult on the phone. Why? Visual cues don't exist; you don't have the gestures, stance, and eye movement which are so important in face-to-face conversation.

Analyze the proposed goal. For example, phone calls involve not only initiating conversation but listening and responding to an unseen speaker as well. Somehow it seems easier to initiate a call than to respond when someone calls you. (Both involve speaking skills, but when you make the call, you control the discussion—at least initially.) Clearly, then, phone calls involve listening skills. Further, they include a cultural component, i.e., appropriate telephone etiquette. "Speak" is obviously not the best verb to choose for our goal—it's just too limiting. So, let's try the word "handle"—it's not razor-sharp, but it is precise enough to connote the feeling you want, broad enough to include speaking, listening, and social rules.

The revised goal then?: "to handle normal telephone conversations." (Note: this is an advanced skill; see the Proficiency Scale at the end of the chapter.)

Now check your work. Have you defined the goal precisely? Ask yourself these questions:

- Does the main action verb describe a specific activity?
- Does the goal state an outcome (rather than a process)?
- Is the outcome stated in terms of your performance?
- Is the goal clear and concise?
- Is the goal important and meaningful, i.e., worth reaching?
- Is the goal realistic and attainable?

Now, let's examine the goal again: *handle* is a bit imprecise, but it includes both speaking and listening, being able to respond when someone calls, being able to call someone and convey your message, and knowing social rules governing telephone conversations. It is broader than "making phone calls" or "answering when people call." It requires **you** to perform (not someone to teach you). The wording emphasizes an outcome. It is also realistic. It gives you an out: "normal" excludes understanding drunks or people with speech impediments or other uncommon situations. Let's go with it.

But wait! The goal seems straightforward, but it's not specific enough. It's not something you can achieve in a day's learning cycle. Let's take the process a step further:

2. Determine appropriate performance objectives.

We have defined a general task. It sets overall direction but covers too much for any given lesson. Let's call our first effort a goal. Now you need more specific achievement indicators. Let's call them performance objectives.

Think in terms of tasks you may want to perform on the telephone. You might, for instance, want to learn to

- request information: asking for a certain item, finding out when the bus leaves.
- convey information: giving directions, describing an event.
- respond to initial words: answering a common phone greeting, identifying yourself, responding to common questions.
- discuss common telephone topics: setting appointments, chit-chatting before giving the telephone to someone else.

Thus, you have further defined learning "to handle normal telephone conversation" to include "requesting and conveying information, responding to common telephone greetings, and participating in common discussion topics."

3. Devise and practice appropriate learning activities.

This step uses the learning cycle: develop specific lessons and practice them until you have mastered them. You might, for instance, work up with your mentor a couple of telephone dialogues and memorize them; drill on the more difficult phrases; practice simulated conversation with your mentor and fellow learners. In place of a wokabaot, you could make several telephone calls to test your ability to use in real conversation the dialogues you have learned. Then, have your mentor ask a friend to call you unannounced.

You have, in short, moved through the practice and communication stages of your daily learning cycle.

4. Evaluate your activities and revise your goals.

With the above example, proof of accomplishment is performance on the telephone—not ability to repeat drills, memorize dialogues, or simulate telephone talk. Now, evaluate your ability to handle real telephone calls. Did you understand what was said to you? Did you provide the requested information? Did you respond with an appropriate greeting and conclude with an appropriate conversation closer?

Handling the phone call is only half the task, however. In goal writing, you test not only your performance but also the appropriateness of the goals themselves. Play goals and performance against each other. Ask yourself these questions:

- Can I perform the tasks as planned?
- Are my learning activities appropriate? (If I master them, will I meet my performance objectives? My overall goal?)
- Do I need additional (or different) learning activities?
- Should I redefine the performance objectives or the goal?

Now, as you evaluate both performance and goal, how does your initial statement hold up? In this case, "to handle normal telephone conversations" seems a reasonable, realistic goal, and the performance objectives you set have helped you to reach the goal.

Goal setting involves continuing definition, action, evaluation, and redefinition. The result is that goals guide you in undertaking appropriate learning activities. Your learning activities in turn help sharpen and clarify your goals. In the process, both activities and goals change.

GUIDELINES FOR LANGUAGE ACHIEVEMENT

For years the Foreign Service Institute (FSI) proficiency scale was the primary test of oral language achievement. Its five-point scale ranked speakers from level 0 (no functional ability) to level 5 (equal to an educated native speaker). The American Council on the Teaching of Foreign Languages (ACTFL) and the Educational Testing Service (ETS) have modified the FSI scale to better classify beginning learners (FSI 0-2).

Both scales present a hierarchy of language skills. Though designed to test speaking proficiency, such scales suggest goals as well as set standards by which to measure achievement. The widely used FSI and ACTFL/ETS scales do, however, tend to view language ability more from the instructor's perspective than the learner's. We have revised them here to meet the needs of the readers of this book more precisely.

Our guide, The Language Learner's Proficiency Scale, consists of two components: a narrative description, which summarizes skill levels, and a self-rating checklist, which suggests performance objectives for each skill level.

The narrative description summarizes your skills. Each statement provides the basic material for defining goals or assessing ability: "can express very simple needs in polite language" (novice — mid); or "can converse on most practical, social, and professional topics" (superior). The narrative description also summarizes your ability to understand and be understood, use proper grammar and pronunciation, and understand the cultural context of a language.

The self-rating checklist contains performance objectives representing clusters of language tasks. The cluster concept is crucial. Each performance objective represents a body of knowledge at each level, not merely the literal translation of specific words. Each is an indicator of achievement, rather than the sum of tasks at each level. We once heard a young learner, for instance, reject the use of a proficiency scale when he noticed the task, "I can make a selection from a menu and order a simple meal." "The scale is irrelevant," he concluded, "because my village doesn't even have a restaurant." He missed the point: each objective represents a concept, a cluster of words and phrases. You pass each level when you master the concept, not when you memorize the local equivalent of the stated objective.

For example, you can master the literal performance objective of "saying hello and goodbye" (novice—low) in the first hour of your first session. As an indicator, however, "hello" represents a cluster of greetings you would learn for different situations: the equivalents of *good morning* (*friend, sir, ma'am*, etc.), *good afternoon, hello, hi, howdy, how ya doin'?, what's up?*, etc.

The Language Learner's Proficiency Scale has two interrelated functions. First, it suggests goals that, when used in concert with the suggestions in this book, provide the basis for setting your own goals. Second, the scale provides benchmarks against which you can evaluate your personal progress.

Use the narrative description to help you assess your overall development. Let it help you define your level of aspiration and analyze your level of achievement. Use the self-rating checklist to identify performance objectives and to measure your language progress.

THE LANGUAGE LEARNER'S PROFICIENCY SCALE

NARRATIVE DESCRIPTION	SELF-RATING CHECKLIST
NOVICE — Low	**NOVICE — Low**

Able to respond to or speak a few isolated words—those borrowed from English, or commonly used, e.g., *gracias, ciao,* etc.

- I can say "hello" and "good-bye."

- I can count to ten.

- I can use courtesy words such as "thank you" and "excuse me."

Has identified him/herself as a language learner.

- I know a handful of words.

- I am eager to begin learning my target language.

- I have set some goals for my language learning.

NOVICE — Mid

NOVICE — Mid

Can express very simple needs in polite language. Uses mostly memorized words and phrases. Can say short phrases if given time to think about what she/he wants to say.

- I can respond to simple commands such as "stand up" and "come here."

- I can greet people and take my leave correctly.

Speaks in a heavy accent with many errors and confuses sounds that are similar.

- I can ask basic questions, using *who, what, when* and *where.*

Speech is difficult to understand,

- I can make simple statements and commands such as "it's hot" even to teachers used to working with language students.

and "turn on the light."

• I can thank people and make simple requests.

• I can use at least fifty words in appropriate contexts.

• I can sing one verse of a folk song or popular sing-along tune.

• I can perform at least one task at the novice-high level.

NOVICE — High

Can ask questions and make simple statements based on memorized sentences. Understands conversation fragments and simple commands. Can deal with simple topics of daily need. Speaks mostly in short, direct sentences, but can say some longer phrases and sentences if given time to think about them first.

Still makes frequent errors in pronunciation and word use. Frequently asks speaker to slow down or repeat. Communicates with coworkers but has difficulty with others.

Behaves considerately in dealing with host country nationals. Understands some nonverbal cues.

NOVICE — High

• I understand and can make simple statements about family, age, address, weather, time, and daily activities.

• I understand some words when the context helps explain them, e.g., in a cafe, the marketplace.

• My vocabulary includes names of basic concepts: days, months, numbers 1-100, articles of clothing, body parts, family relationships.

• I can use at least one hundred nouns and verbs in appropriate contexts.

• I am beginning to know what's expected of me in simple social situations.

• I can perform at least two tasks at the intermediate—low level.

INTERMEDIATE — Low

Can speak on familiar topics, ask and answer simple questions, initiate and respond to simple statements, and carry on face-to-face discussions. Can pick out the main idea in a friendly informal conversation.

Often speaks incorrectly but by repeating, generally can be understood by native speakers who regularly deal with foreigners.

Frequently can understand native speaker if he/she repeats or speaks more slowly.

INTERMEDIATE — Low

• I can initiate and close conversations appropriately.

• I can introduce myself or someone else.

• I can buy a ticket, catch a bus or train, and get off at the right place.

• I can respond to simple directions from customs officials, policemen, or other officials.

• I can discuss simple topics with friends.

INTERMEDIATE — Mid

Can participate in simple conversations about some survival needs and social traditions. Can discuss topics beyond basic survival, such as personal history and leisure time activities.

Beginning to use correct basic grammar constructions such as subject-verb and noun-adjective agreement.

INTERMEDIATE — Mid

• I can handle questions about my marital status, nationality, occupation, age, and place of birth.

• I can order a simple meal from a restaurant menu.

• I can ask for or tell the time, date, and day of the week.

• I can handle simple business at the post office, a bank, and the drugstore.

• I'm beginning to speak more correctly; my subjects and verbs generally agree.

• I can perform at least one task at the intermediate—high level.

INTERMEDIATE — High

Can participate in short conversations about most survival needs, limited social conventions, and other topics. Gets the gist of conversations on familiar topics, though finds it hard to tune in on long conversations or in unfamiliar situations.

Speaks mostly in short, discrete sentences, but shows occasional bursts of spontaneity. Can use most question forms, basic tenses, pronouns, and verb inflections, though still speaks with many errors.

Can be understood by native speakers used to speaking with foreigners. By repeating things, can frequently be understood by the general public.

In dealing with host country citizens, can get along in familiar survival situations and with native speakers accustomed to foreigners.

INTERMEDIATE — High

• I can buy my basic foodstuffs, rent a hotel room, and bargain when appropriate.

• I can talk about my favorite pastimes or sports.

• I can describe how to get from here to places like the post office, a restaurant, or a local tourist attraction.

• I can talk about things that happened in the past or might happen in the future.

• I can carry on simple conversations with native speakers who are used to dealing with foreigners.

• I can perform at least two of the tasks at the advanced level.

ADVANCED

Can participate in most casual and some work conversations. Can give simple directions or explanations at work. Can talk about past and future events. With a minimum of repetition and rewording, can get the gist of normal conversation by native speakers.

ADVANCED

• I can describe my work in some detail and discuss with my co-workers most work-related tasks.

• I can talk comfortably about topics of general interest, such as the weather and current events.

• I can deal with and explain

Vocabulary is good enough to speak simply with only a few circumlocutions and can speak extemporaneously on many topics. Accent clearly that of a learner, but can generally be understood.

unexpected problems, such as losing my traveler's checks.

• I can take and give messages by telephone.

• I can be understood by most native speakers, and I can follow normal conversations involving native speakers.

• I can perform at least one task at the advanced plus level.

ADVANCED PLUS

Can handle most work requirements and conversations on topics of particular interest. Can express facts, give instructions, describe, report, and talk about current, past, and future activities.

Often speaks fluently and easily, though occasionally pauses to think of a word. Continues to make some grammatical errors.

In dealing with native speakers, understands common rules of etiquette, taboos and sensitivities, and handles routine social situations when dealing with people accustomed to foreigners.

ADVANCED PLUS

• I can hire an employee, discuss qualifications, duties, hours, and pay in my new language.

• I can instruct a coworker on how to perform a common task.

• I can give opinions, facts, and explain points of view.

• I can talk with ease about my past, my current activities, and what I hope to do in the future.

• I generally speak easily and fluently with only minor pauses.

• I can make culturally acceptable requests, accept or refuse invitations, apologize, and offer and receive gifts.

• I can perform at least two of the tasks at the superior level.

SUPERIOR

Can converse on most practical, social, and professional topics. Can deal with unfamiliar topics, provide explanations, resolve problems, describe in detail, offer supported opinions, and hypothesize. Beginning to talk about abstract ideas.

Rarely has to grope for a word. Control of grammar is good and errors almost never bother the native speaker.

Can participate appropriately in most social and work situations. Understands most nonverbal responses; beginning to understand culture-related humor.

SUPERIOR

• I can carry out most work assignments in the target language.

• I can handle routine social situations with ease.

• I can participate effectively in most general discussions involving native speakers.

• I can handle normal telephone conversations.

• I can listen to a radio program, oral report, or speech and take accurate notes.

• I can deal with an unexpected problem or a social blunder.

• I can support my opinions in a discussion or argument.

• I am beginning to understand jokes and word play.

• I seldom have to ask speakers to repeat or explain.

• I can speak at a normal rate of speed, without groping for words or trying to avoid complex grammatical structures.

DISTINGUISHED

Can use the language fluently and accurately on all levels of professional need. Can tailor language to fit the audience: counsel, persuade, negotiate, represent a point

DISTINGUISHED

• I can carry out any job responsibility in my second language.

• I can speak appropriately to a professional group, my staff, a of view, and interpret for dignitaries.

Speaks with only rare pronunciation or grammar errors.

Picks up on most nonverbal cues; understands humor and most allusions. Behaves in a culturally appropriate manner in a range of social and professional settings.

government official, a friend, the elderly and children.

• I can act as an interpreter at a professional meeting or function.

• I rarely make pronunciation or grammar errors.

• I always understand native speakers, even when they are talking to each other.

• I can participate in joking, including puns and word play.

• I can read cultural gestures, body language and facial expressions accurately.

NATIVE COMPETENCE

Functions as would an educated native speaker.

NATIVE COMPETENCE

• I am equally as fluent in my second language as in English.

• I have command of idioms, colloquialisms, and historical and literary allusions.

• I am well-versed on the history, beliefs, customs, politics, and geography of the host country.

• I am completely at ease culturally in any social or professional setting.

Four

Community: *Utilizing the Living Classroom*

A community is a group of people who live close to one another. It may be a village, small town, neighborhood, or a section of a city. Its structures include places where its residents live, and sometimes shops and police stations, streets or paths and places of worship. Its people have language, laws, values and beliefs, and history.

Communities consist mostly of insiders, the people who live there; they understand community life, its unwritten codes, its taboos, its definition of what is acceptable and unacceptable. Some community members can explain those rules; many can not—they just "know" what is right and wrong. They act accordingly.

Communities offer absolutely marvelous classrooms for the language learner. As both language learner and an outsider, you need to learn how to participate in community life as would an insider, in cultural behavior as well as in language. In situ learning encourages you to tackle both simultaneously. The interplay of language learning and personal involvement speeds language acquisition, which in turn fosters more involvement. Cast aside the image of studying a language and the people who speak it; rather, learn culture and language by immersing yourself in both. Participation in community life builds language; language enables participation. They support each other.

You won't become a true insider in your new community, but you can become accepted, comfortable, and adept at living by rules which insiders take for granted. View yourself as standing at one end of a continuum that leads from outsider to insider. At your side is your mentor, that special person who is your language and cultural guide. As you learn, you move closer to the insider end of that continuum. This chapter suggests a framework for speeding you on your journey.

It offers first a perspective on your new community, a way of observing it so that you more quickly make sense of it. Second, it suggests approaches that help you find the doors through which you can enter and participate as an insider.

PERSPECTIVES FOR UNDERSTANDING A COMMUNITY

Communities are made up of people, but definite patterns of living identify them just as fingerprints identify an individual. To begin to understand your community, study what people and institutions do and how they relate to each other. This lets you concentrate on smaller pieces of a complex system.

You don't have to be in-country or speak your target language fluently to begin exploring your community. Part of your preparation for living abroad should include a basic review of your host country's history, current events, cultural norms. Even if you read well in your target language, a good English overview of your host country's history will provide an English-speaking perspective useful in discussion. If available, you should also obtain a cross-cultural manual that discusses host country customs and norms as they contrast with those of Americans (see Supplementary Readings for this chapter, p. 145). Such background will help you formulate questions in the target language that will verify, elaborate, or modify your perceptions of the country and its customs. Once you are in-country, ask the cultural affairs officer at a U.S. embassy or consulate for a reading list, as well as materials that summarize host country laws as they apply to expatriates.

Look at your community from the perspectives listed below. Each offers a different window on community life; each provides different questions to ask yourself about how society is organized. Begin with those that seem most interesting, most accessible, or best match your personality and background.

These perspectives suggest topics around which specific language lessons may be developed. Some learners have a preference for these kinds of general topics. Others find it useful to concentrate on the incidents of everyday life. No matter what your preference, however, your learning will come from day-to-day interactions with individual people.

1. Work and occupations: what people do for a living and how they do it.

How do people earn a living? What work do men do? Women? What positions are held in high esteem? How are people compensated for their work? What relationships exist between employers and employees?

Visit with people as they work. Ask them to describe their activities as they show you how they do them. This can be particularly enlightening if you are in a society in which basic living makes up the day's work— finding, cutting, and preparing building materials; building and repairing houses; fishing; farming; gathering or hunting food; hauling water; preparing meals; cleaning house; rearing children; making the essentials for daily life, such as tools, furniture, canoes, cloth, totems, etc. In cities skilled laborers have a wealth of information on technical subjects. Talk to the mechanics, carpenters, masons, printers, and bakers about their work.

2. Social relations: how people carry out the routine activities that complement their work lives.

How do people spend their leisure and recreational time? What games, events, entertainment are common?

What religions predominate? What religious customs and beliefs are common? How do people observe religious holidays? What associations, clubs, groupings exist? What do they do? Who belongs?

How do people deal with sickness and health? Is there an indigenous system of healers (which may coexist with a Western medical system)? What help exists for the poor, disabled, handicapped?

What ceremonies or formalities are observed with initiations and rites of passage, such as birth, puberty, graduation, marriage, death? On what occasions do people give gifts? To whom?

What rules govern relationships among different people, including family members, men and women, elderly and young, leaders and followers? How do people relate to each other as friends and visitors, as competitors or enemies?

Join in leisure activities, social events, ceremonies. Attend meetings of clubs, organizations, and church services. Observe how people treat each other. Try to identify actions, words, and/or symbols that accompany interaction between different types of people. Find out what provisions are made for people who are "different" and how people cope with illness, distress, misfortune.

3. Government: how people govern themselves.

What bodies govern at the national, state or provincial, regional, city, local levels? How do the responsibilities of ministries, legislatures, and councils differ? How do courts and law enforcement agencies function, including traditional or customary ways of dealing with violators of tribal or ethnic mores? How are laws made and enforced, and crimes punished? What acts are defined as a crime? How do people become leaders—election, family heritage, land ownership or wealth? What roles do political parties play in government? What are the roles and positions of public servants and bureaucrats?

If permitted, observe government in action: legislatures and councils, courts and local government bodies. Learn the names of the major ministries or government bureaus and their areas of responsibility. Find out legal expectations of you as a foreigner. In particular, make sure you meet any requirements to report your whereabouts; obtain permits, licenses, certificates, or passes; or fill out forms. See if you can find a summary of laws which might govern you as a foreigner, particularly those dealing with alcohol and drug use, currency exchange, residency and employment, accidents and illness.

Try to understand the major legislative issues as well as controversial issues arousing group protest, newspaper editorials and media commentary. Become conversant with what people argue about and discuss over coffee, tea, and the local brew.

4. Education and child care: how the society transmits its knowledge and values and takes care of its children.

What educational institutions exist, from preschool through university and adult education, public and private? Who participates in formal education programs? What is the country's rate of literacy? What roles do various people have in education, for example, teachers and administrators, parents, students and other citizens? How highly regarded are educators and educational certification?

Compare your educational system with that of the host country. If you are a student, the educational system provides ready-made discussion topics—typical course loads, types of exams, role of the student in the classroom, teaching methodologies, student involvement in educational decision making.

What does the society expect of its children? What is the proper way to raise and train children? Who is responsible for child rearing? Spend time with parents and their children. Observe methods of discipline, expectations for behavior, participation in household chores, training, interaction between parents and children, and between other adults and children.

5. Country history and culture: past and current development.

What dates, sites, historical figures, events, leaders, and problems are important in the nation's history? What artifacts attest to the country's past? Where are they displayed? What stories, legends, fables, and myths describe its history? What ethnic, tribal, religious or geographically defined groups exist, and how do they relate to one another?

Visit shrines, museums, monuments, revered sites. Learn the names of important people and events celebrated in books, films, songs, and art work. If your language ability permits, read works by the country's masters, enroll in a literature appreciation, history, or political science class. Attend lectures and discussions. Listen to the local storytellers. Observe styles of dress, cuisine, marketplace activities, folk art and crafts that identify different groups. Vacation in different parts of the country to see, firsthand, different living styles. Listen to (but don't repeat) the ethnic jokes that identify groups that may be looked down upon or discriminated against.

6. Development: the country in world economics and politics.

What is the country's relation to its neighbors, to former colonial powers or former colonies, to other nations? What is its ability to meet the needs for food, shelter, medical care, education, its people's aspirations? Does the country in general govern its own affairs? Is it largely dependent upon the actions of other countries? What are its development strategies and projects, its assistance programs?

Learn about the country's products and trading partners, its balance of trade. Find out how it votes on major issues considered in the United Nations. Learn what impact the policies and practices of the U.S. have on the country and how host country citizens view them. Try to see the U.S. from the perspective of host country citizens. Find out about major development projects, aid programs, hopes for the future.

7. Artifacts: the things that people have.

What things do people have? What materials, styles, and uses can be attributed to dwellings, business places, public buildings? What music, arts, crafts are common? How are they a part of everyday living? What special functions do they perform?

Observe clothing, food, household belongings and decorations, personal adornment, tools. Find out about major cultural groups and the styles and artifacts associated with them. Identify art forms. Find out about items featured on stamps, coins, in art exhibits.

8. Natural environment: land and its nonhuman inhabitants.

What is the physical layout of the land? How do people view the land, that is, its importance, conservation and use, ownership? How does the existence or lack of particular natural resources affect the society and its actions, for example, the topography (rivers, mountains, the ocean, jungles, deserts) and the climate (typhoons, monsoons, snow storms, drought, extreme heat or cold)? What plants and animals inhabit the country? What are their uses, treatment, roles in society? Are certain animals or plants accorded special significance or given special treatment? Why?

Visit game parks, zoos, aquariums, and botanical gardens to understand the variety of the country's nonhuman inhabitants and to get a sense of how they are treated. Find out about major crops and agricultural techniques. Be alert to the use of animals in agriculture, industry, transportation.

Let's turn now to a perspective that can help you open doors to participation in community life and language learning.

REACHING INTO THE COMMUNITY

View the community as consisting of at least four concentric circles of helpers—people who, in different positions and for different reasons, will be your instructors in the natural community classroom.[1]

• At the core of these circles are your **mentors**, with whom you will work closely. These are special relationships. We will explore them fully later in the chapter.

• The second circle consists of **family and intimate friends**, who will provide basic support. They may be members of your host family, coworkers or fellow students with whom you spend your days, or other close friends. Aside from your mentor, they know you better than anyone in-country.

• The third circle is made up of your **network of regular contacts**, people you see frequently, usually in particular locations—in the marketplace, at meeting places, on your way to work. As you develop a regular walking route through a neighborhood, you begin to recognize people, and they you. You become part of their daily routine. They may be individuals—a shopkeeper, the man who sits on his porch, a vendor—or they may be groups: the guys who hang out at the barbershop, the morning coffee klatsch at Ni Song Cafe, the Parcheesi players in the square. They may be acquaintances, friends of friends. They are the "regulars." At first, they offer discussion related to the specific situation, perhaps conversation about their shop or work or clientele, or about the grandchild who plays beside the house. Later, as your acquaintanceship grows, so do the possible topics.

• The final circle consists of **strangers**. They are people from different walks of life, different age groups, men and women, married and single, people of higher and lesser status. As Larson notes: "[Strangers] provide a great opportunity to stretch.... You are forced to use language in new ways.... It is where you get ordinary people to help you learn their language. Nothing is more important in language learning."[2]

From each circle you will find native speakers whose skills and perspectives bring different windows to the language. Your work with your mentor, with your family and intimate friends, and with the network you establish allows you to build from a structured, controlled situation to one of great variation and unpredictability. Only a real community provides the milieu for such learning.

These circles of helpers open the doors to a community's potential as a living classroom. You don't learn only from a mentor or a family member or people from your network of contacts. Rather, your daily learning cycle taps the resources offered in all of these circles. People from your network of contacts help your language grow around particular topics, in areas of their special interest or expertise. Family and friends enable you to talk about personal needs, relationships, personal insights into living in their society. Your mentor will help you bridge the gaps, broaden your understanding and ability, focus your learning on particular needs. Strangers test your preparation and introduce you to new subjects and ideas.

It is with a mentor, however, that you most quickly focus your language learning. The rest of the chapter will define more clearly the mentor concept. We will discuss qualities of a good mentor; selection, compensation, and training; and suggestions on how a mentor relationship works.

Keep in mind, however, that while discussion is phrased in terms of a mentor, the suggestions apply broadly to working with any native speaker in a planned language-learning atmosphere.

THE MENTOR RELATIONSHIP

A mentorship is a relationship in which a language learner plans and directs learning experiences which are guided by a native speaker. In a mentorship, the native speaker agrees to assist a learner in an organized, learner-directed program of language acquisition.

In a mentorship, the **learner**

- sets long-term learning goals and daily objectives;
- determines the content of each lesson or study period;
- plans specific learning events, including language exercises;
- trains the mentor in techniques that best fit the learner's individual learning style.

The **mentor**

- serves as the primary language role model, that is, the speaker whose voice the learner initially mimics for pronunciation, tone, phrasing, etc.;

- develops basic dialogues and passages that capture the essence of the learner's meaning in locally acceptable language;
- conducts drills and exercises that enable the learner to master basic dialogues and passages;
- develops and conducts exercises and drills to correct common mistakes or language misuse;
- identifies learner errors and corrects them; and
- evaluates learner performance in relation to his/her goals.

A good mentor/learner relationship exhibits some of the qualities of a good teacher/student relationship. Yet, it also differs sharply—in a mentor/learner relationship, the learner, not the mentor, provides fundamental direction. The mentor assists by interpreting language goals and content in the local context and by guiding the learner in reaching those goals. In this, the mentor follows. But the mentor also leads by designing appropriate drills, correcting behavior, and suggesting exercises and tasks.

A good mentor isn't merely a translator; at times she rejects the suggestions of the learner, offers alternatives, pushes the learner in different directions. She is forceful enough to disagree, to point out errors; skilled enough to dream up alternatives; clever enough to keep lessons moving, varied, interesting; observant enough to know when to repeat, when to press, when to step back.

A good mentor is a guide and interpreter beyond direct language learning. She understands your new community and its culture. She understands how language use fits that culture and uses your lessons to deepen your cultural understanding. She points out cues that you as a beginning learner cannot see or hear. She interprets actions that you have missed but that have conveyed important meaning to others. She plays important social roles beyond that of a teacher: your passport to events, gatherings, discussions open only to insiders; the legitimizer of your presence in special places; the interpreter who smoothes over your indiscretions, ill-chosen remarks, unintentional offenses; the explainer of your behavior to bewildered country mates.

A good mentor/learner relationship requires time together. It means cooperative planning. It involves listening to each other, trying to communicate despite language and cultural differences. It means building a close working relationship, training each other, and agreeing on ground rules based on mutual respect and trust.

The mentor/learner relationship described above is the ideal, a goal, a concept. Sometimes the relationship will be embodied in a single person. If you develop such a relationship, rejoice, for beyond your language learning you will have developed a friendship you will never forget. Unfortunately, human relationships only occasionally reach the ideal. More likely, you will develop friendships with several people, each of whom will have some of the characteristics of an ideal mentor. If so, rejoice as well, for your learning will prosper as your friendships increase.

We portray the ideal here, not because your mentor/learner relationship must mirror the ideal before the in situ concept works, but because the ideal defines parameters. Recognize that your goal is to identify and work with native speakers who can help you learn your target language. Any relationship that does that for you will be a successful one.

SELECTING YOUR MENTOR

Ideally, mentor selection is easy. Your mentor finds you. As you work with people, mix socially, make friends and contacts, you will meet potential mentors. The mentor relationship occurs naturally and spontaneously. But it takes time.

Regrettably, not everyone can spend two years overseas. If you are a summer-abroad student, a seasonal fugitive from Midwestern winters, or simply someone itching to get on with it, you will need to find a mentor much more rapidly. Here are some tactics (not mutually exclusive) to speed up the process:

1. Arrange to take language lessons. Identify a teacher through your school, work, a local college or secondary school, or just by asking around. Suggest a short program, outline your expectations, and agree on terms. This begins your language study and the lessons open up the opportunity to find a mentor in your instructor or among that person's friends.

2. Discuss your desire for language learning with a local English-speaking intermediary (a school official, coworker, etc.), explain the mentor concept to your contact, and ask that person to suggest someone. Proceed with caution, though. Your intermediary may be embarrassed or offended if the arrangement doesn't work out. Explain this approach carefully. Emphasize the difference between a mentor and a traditional teacher. (If it seems appropriate, have your contact read this chapter). Request a tentative arrangement so that both you and the prospective mentor have a chance to try each other out. Then, hope for the best!

3. Select housing that increases the likelihood you will find a mentor. If you stay with a family, for instance, look for a family with some-

one about your same age and sex, or a family willing to help you identify a mentor.

A mentor relationship is special. Nurture it carefully; let it grow gradually. Yet, begin language study as soon as possible. Begin with the caveat that you and your initial helper may have to end the arrangement if it doesn't pan out.

PROFILE OF A LANGUAGE MENTOR

"What kind of person makes a good mentor?" you ask. In a nutshell, one who is patient, understanding, supportive, creative, knowledgeable, firm but fair, bright—all the qualities one would want in any ordinary superhero. More realistically, look for the following qualities, realizing that you may not find them all in a single person.

Personal compatibility. A mentor/learner relationship is an intimate one. If your mentor/learner relationship is successful, your mentor will become a valued friend, perhaps your closest.

Look for what you would want in a friendship—trust, respect, confidence, companionship. Look for shared interests. Your relationship will be close; you must be at ease with one another, comfortable in being together.

Local ties. The in situ approach rests upon your desire to use the target language locally. To build ties to the local community, your mentor needs a personal network of friends and acquaintances. Tap that network to hasten your entry into the community and the language.

Chances are, your first prospects for a mentor will be someone without such a network. Most likely you will develop rapport with young professionals, educated, articulate men and women who themselves may be newcomers to the community (public school teachers, ministers and priests, young government officials, people whose residence follows their employment). Don't automatically embrace them as mentors. Weigh that immediate rapport against the importance of a local network. Nor should you automatically exclude them; weigh the importance of a local network against their other positive qualities.

Teaching ability. In general, mentors are neither formal language instructors nor certified teachers. If your target language is a regional language or dialect, formal teachers may not exist. Certified teachers may not view a dialect or regional language as proper. Most teachers of major languages have been trained to teach **about** language, explain grammar rules, describe usage. While that knowledge may at times be useful, more often it hinders learning.

On the other hand, don't automatically exclude a teacher who has the qualities of a good mentor. A teacher who can identify with the methodology of independent, learner-guided instruction will recognize the value of this approach, even though it conflicts with his formal training. An experienced teacher may have the ability to develop dialogues and drills, supervise language exercises, identify and correct errors, suggest appropriate learning activities, and evaluate your progress.

A good mentor will know when and how to correct your errors, as well as follow the path you lay out for language study. You will make many errors, in pronunciation, word order, grammar, etc. Your tongue won't fit everything you want to say in the order you want to say it. Your brain won't remember at the proper moment all it has learned. You will try to formulate sentences that can't be constructed in the language. You will try to translate thoughts that have no direct translation or say things that aren't said in polite conversation.

You want a mentor who tells you of your mistakes, someone who corrects you, disagrees with you—but who does so in a constructive, positive way. It's essential that your mentor help you learn from your mistakes. This isn't always easy. It may be difficult to find mentors who can transcend cultural barriers to provide straightforward correction, particularly if you are older, or if your position, skills, or education carries status in the community. Young persons in particular may be extremely deferential toward their elders or outsiders like you. Empathize, for instance, with our friend whose otherwise excellent mentor could not bring himself to play his role fully. For a year the learner thought he had been cheerfully requesting his mentor to "walk back and forth." Alas, he had been calling him "a vagina." (A fellow expatriate, not his mentor, finally pointed out his mistake in diction.)

If in your host country the culture prohibits people from directly contradicting or correcting others, you may have to attune yourself to more subtle messages of correction. No matter how it is done, however, your mentor must be able to point out errors and help you correct them.

Availability. Language learning is time-consuming. You won't become fluent by studying hurriedly twice a week for an hour between work and dinner. Your mentor must have the time to commit to long hours on a regular basis.

Sex. Customs governing relationships between men and women vary. In many countries, especially those of the Third World, it is important to be sure that females are not put into compromising situations by being alone with a man in closed quarters. You can avoid any misunderstanding, of course, by choosing a mentor of the same sex, though in doing so you obviously limit the pool of potential mentors available to you.

The risk in working with a peer of the opposite sex, or in a man's case, with a younger female, is not only that it might develop into a forbidden sexual relationship but that the relationship may be **perceived** by community members as sexual, which can be just as damaging. In general, if language sessions between mentors and learners of the opposite sex occur in highly visible public places where others are present (such as open school offices), misinterpretation by a mentor's peers and the community at large can be avoided. Be sure to check local custom. As with any male-female friendship, however, the physical, intellectual, and social closeness of the mentor relationship can lead to sexual liaison. Much can be said for learning language from one's lover, but the mentor relationship proposed here does not encompass lovers.

With a modicum of discretion, you should be able to work effectively with a mentor of the opposite sex. The keys to success are understanding local customs, being attuned to public perceptions of your relationships, and clearly understanding your own feelings and behavior.

COMMUNICATING WITH A MENTOR

Do good mentors speak English? Some do. Others don't. If you are fortunate, you will have the chance to work with both. Each presents different challenges and opportunities.

We prefer to work with monolinguals, i.e., non-English speakers. Though at times communication may be difficult with a monolingual mentor—it's particularly more challenging initially explaining general concepts such as dialogue preparation and drilling techniques—the fact that your mentor doesn't speak English forces you to conduct your sessions in the target language. The inability to divert sessions into English or to chat about the U.S. or your impressions of the host country preserves language learning as the focus of your sessions. It sharpens your communicative creativity. You must use gestures, sign language, and/or alternate phrasing to get your points across.

If you have difficulty communicating the basic ideas of in situ methodology to your monolingual mentor, call on an English-speaking intermediary to help you out. If you are working with a monolingual mentor, you will want to read the articles cited in the references for this chapter.

The advantage of working with a bilingual mentor is that you can more easily explain your expectations and the learning cycle, particularly at the beginning, as you develop a working relationship. The ease of communication may make you feel more comfortable and make learning less stressful, but be sure you guard against (1) **talking about** the language rather than talking in it; (2) translating, except as a last resort; (3) asking **why** native speakers say something rather than accepting it as fact and concentrating on language practice.

If you work with a bilingual mentor, you can minimize the natural inclination to lapse into English by making a pact to speak only in the target language, by agreeing to limit the mentor's use of English to **listening** rather than speaking, or by agreeing to limit use of English to certain activities, particular hours, or certain days of the week.

In short, a mentor's ability or inability to speak English is not the crucial question. What is important is how you best utilize his or her abilities. Neither is better; they are simply different.

WHAT COMPENSATION FOR A MENTOR?

Your mentor may be overjoyed with your progress. Her friends may marvel at her ability to help such an awkwardly speaking foreigner master the sounds local folks take for granted. Yet, while great reward may exist for her in knowing that she has done a difficult job well, your mentor's compensation ought to be more than pride. Make it commensurate with the time, devotion, skill, and ability she contributes to your progress.

"Then I should pay my mentor?" you ask.

"Yes," we reply, "but in a locally accepted manner."

You might contract to pay in cash by the hour, week, or month. Find out from your mentor or intermediary if direct payment is appropriate locally. If it is, pay directly, but negotiate the rate and the frequency through an intermediary. That removes the buyer/seller roles from the mentor relationship. If direct payment is inappropriate, explore other options: give cash to another family member; give gifts on appropriate occasions; pay for some other event, for example, money to help with a baptism celebration; give English lessons to a friend or family member; arrange separate English classes for your mentor.

Many are the possibilities for tangible as well as psychological payment to a mentor. Explore them. Your rewards will be great; so should your mentor's.

DEFINING THE MENTOR'S ROLE

As a self-directed learner you are both student and trainer. You must convey your learning needs to your mentor so that she can guide your learning. Because this will be a new role for her, you must demonstrate it clearly. Just as you the learner must repeat lessons previously learned, so must you the trainer repeat the major points your mentor needs to know. You can't simply explain what you want once, then lean back and relax while your mentor chauffeurs you on a perfect journey. She, like you, needs to practice the fundamentals from time to time.

It is critical that you train your mentor experientially, that is, that she practice the techniques rather than just hear you lecture about them. You'll need to demonstrate the learning cycle concept to her, show her what you expect to happen in your sessions, involve her in developing passages and conducting drills, etc. You'll have to begin by being a creative teacher rather than a learner. If you are yourself a beginning learner, you may wish to involve a bilingual third party who can make sure your mentor understands the concepts and techniques (and to foster, as much as possible, the notion that your relationship with your mentor will be conducted in the target language rather than English). If you are a beginner working with a monolingual mentor, a third party who can help you establish a basis of understanding will greatly facilitate your early lessons. If you have some facility in the target language, attempt your training in that language.

At a minimum, train your mentor in the following areas.

1. Dialogue and passage development. Practice constructing passages based on a general image of what you want to convey. Use a cross-cultural exercise. Ask your mentor (in the target language if you can) to imagine life in the United States. Have her describe what she thinks a simple encounter (meeting your parents, going shopping, or enrolling in a college class) would be like. Jot down her description, noting phrases that don't quite sound right.

Then, develop a passage that captures the intent of your mentor's description in grammatically and culturally correct English. Point out how your sentences differ from those used by the mentor. Next, based on your English passage, have your mentor help you construct a similar passage in the target language. As you develop the dialogue, compare the differences between it and the English language dialogue.

As a summary, reiterate that a passage should convey the *sense* of an idea rather than a word-for-word translation. Emphasize that the mentor's job is to help translate the learner's thoughts into the target language.

2. Drilling techniques. Practice conducting drills such as those in chapter 2. Training should include actual practice in drilling. If you speak a third language, use it for the drills rather than English or the host country language. Practice in an unknown language gives your mentor an intuitive feel for how drills work and a better sense of the need for extensive repetition. Lead your mentor through a full range of drills, modeling the pace, style, and speed that you prefer for your own learning.

3. Role play. Practice different roles from several role plays. Try role-playing (in English) a mentor preparing a host country national for a trip to the U.S. Develop passages involving a clerk in a drug store, a used car salesman, a teacher assigning a group report, or some other situation that conveys typical American settings that are different from the host country. Outline a situation, develop a dialogue, and practice. Exchange roles and let your mentor lead as well as participate in the role plays.

4. Analysis. Practice critiquing performance and identifying areas that need additional work.

After you have acted out several role plays, critique them. Compare how Americans and your hosts react in each situation. Identify possible behavioral differences—an employee's stance when talking informally to his employer; gestures that convey meaning; sentence structures that denote informality. Note how sentence structures, gestures, and stance might change if the same employee were speaking to a high-ranking executive at a formal meeting. Then, analyze your role plays of the host country equivalents of similar situations. Encourage your mentor to tell you when your behavior isn't the same as local behavior.

5. Cultural cues. Practice identifying cultural behaviors reflected in language. Identify a situation in which host country nationals appear to behave differently from Americans. (Use care not to imply that either behavior is better, or more natural, or preferred—just that people from different cultures behave differently.) Prepare a dialogue representing American behavior and language in the situation. Begin with something simple and nonthreatening. If, for example, host community people buy fresh food in a market, role-play a shopping trip to an American supermarket. Ask your role-playing partner to describe how you find a particular cut of meat, for example, by selecting it from an open counter rather than having it cut for you; by paying a posted price rather than bargaining for it.

Or pretend to be an American worker talking to his employer. You chat as friends; you diplomatically criticize something the boss has done; you correct his mistake. Though your mentor may find it difficult to perform such a role, encourage her to handle the situation as an American would. Practice the exercise several times, then discuss the concept of culturally different behavior. Explain that just as she (in the role play) had to alter her natural behavior to conform to an unnatural American cultural pattern in the role play, you hope that she will teach you to behave in a locally acceptable manner in similar situations.

6. Correction. Practice identifying and correcting mistakes.

As language learners we want native speakers to identify errors and correct us. In some societies such direct comment may be considered culturally insensitive; interpersonal relations are handled with deft subtlety to avoid offending others. What you may view as frankness may be perceived by your mentor and friends to be brutally tactless. In such societies, direct face-to-face correction may be impossible. And merely exhorting your mentor to correct you may be ineffective. (Your plea, "Please be frank with me!" makes as much sense as your mentor telling you, in English, "Please be impolite to me!") Sometimes, discussing the cultural difference involved will help. Often, you will need to convey through action rather than exhortation that correction can help you. As you gain language facility, occasionally slip a phrase you know to be incorrect into your practice sessions. Then, subtly inquire at an appropriate moment whether you used the phrase correctly or if there might be a better usage for that situation.

You may, on the other hand, find a mentor who loves to correct you, one whose corrections make it impossible for you to complete a sentence unscathed. Nothing breaks your train of thought faster than constant correction. It may just be a matter of training or explanation. Ask your mentor to wait until the conversation is over to offer correction, or even jot down corrections to make at a later time. Explain and/or demonstrate how to make corrections supportively. If your mentor's corrections continue to be a stream of putdowns with no positive support, find a different mentor.

THE MECHANICS OF A LEARNING RELATIONSHIP

You have found your mentor. Your training sessions have been enjoyable and productive. You work together regularly. The following suggestions will make your sessions even more productive.

1. Lay out clear expectations for each day's activities.

Your daily sessions require planning and preparation. Make sure you and your mentor understand the day's plan. Meet regularly at specified times and locations, not when you "find the time" or have the inclination. To have productive sessions, both you and your mentor must view them as important.

Early on, establish a normal routine for each day's activities. For starters, try the following:

- an overview of today's activities,
- review of yesterday's main points, including role plays of the main passage,

- review of major drills in yesterday's session,
- construction of a new passage,
- formal pattern drills on the new passage,
- a series of role plays,
- community wokabaot,
- wokabaot evaluation,
- follow-up drills and passage revision as needed,
- brief discussion of possible topics for the next session,
- suggested activities to prepare for the next session.

2. Conduct serious, hard-working sessions.

Nothing destroys sustained learning more quickly than getting together with a mentor, having a good time, and never getting around to language instruction. At first it seems enjoyable, but both of you will quickly become dissatisfied because of the waste of time.

The point can't be overemphasized. As your friendship deepens, it becomes increasingly difficult to stay on task; you find you have too much to share. One tack is to respond to your mentor's questions about you, your background, interests, thoughts (and your wish to know your mentor better) by discussing them in the target language. Simply build those topics into your learning cycles.

If your mentor wants to chat in English, resist! If your mentor wishes to practice English, set her up with a fellow expatriate who can be her English mentor. If a fellow expatriate is also studying the language with a mentor, perhaps you can arrange to guide your compatriot's mentor in English, and vice versa.

If that is not possible, arrange separate sessions. In one, you are the mentor and you help your friend learn English. In the other, your mentor guides you in her language. Keep your respective mentor and learner roles (and your English and host country language usage) separate. Not to do so is to confuse the roles and torpedo your learner/mentor relationship.

3. Vary your session activities and techniques.

Variety alleviates boredom and increases your study effectiveness. Vary your daily activities. This is not to recommend a grab bag of exercises plucked at random from some handy activities kit, but planned, goal-oriented tasks done in a variety of interesting ways. Language learning, while hard work, shouldn't be excruciatingly painful. You should enjoy it.

4. Respond to creativity and variation.

Encourage, use and build on your mentor's ideas and creativity. If you have chosen well, your mentor will offer variations that enhance and enliven your study.

Remain ever vigilant, of course, to assure that your language activities lead toward the goals you have set.

5. Remember those cultural differences.

As your friendship grows, it will become increasingly difficult to remember that you and your mentor come from different societies. You will find times when you ache to confide in her, to express your frustration and homesickness, to lament the times you have been misunderstood, to let out pent-up irritations with her country and its people. Especially during those low times when culture shock is most intense, you will want to turn to someone who knows and cares about you.

Remember, though, that your mentor is on her home ground; she is not an American. No matter how close or how empathetic, her perspective is derived from her own culture and country. The kind of stereotyping, denigrating, and ridiculing of host cultures which often provides emotional catharsis for people under cross-cultural stress will be unacceptable to her.

Individual friendship can transcend cultural chasms. Yet, the very closeness that friendship creates opens us to hurting one another deeply. Friendship stretches the latitude we have to express ourselves. But it also constricts our ability to express ourselves freely. A flippant remark, an offhand, "Gee, I wish I had a job like yours so I could come to work at ten..." has been enough to shatter a budding intercultural friendship.

In many ways cross-cultural sensitivity is made easier when all around you is totally foreign. It doesn't take a wizard to realize while sitting in a campfire-lit community meeting in a village of leaf houses that, as the only white person among black Melanesians, the only English speaker among Kwaio speakers, that you are dealing with a different culture.

But when you are sitting in a modern chair in a modern office, talking with people who dress like you and speak English as well as you do, it is easy to forget that you come from different cultures. Indeed, the very ease with which you communicate can be a danger. Meaning is in the minds of the speaker and the listener, not only in the words. Even when using a common language, if the cultural contexts of the minds are different, miscommunication and misunderstanding may still result.

As your relationship with your mentor deepens, remember that despite your increasing ability to communicate through language, cultural differences remain that need to be attended to.

---

[1]This perspective on community residents is adapted from the work of Don Larson, presented in *Guidelines for Barefoot Language Learning*, 1984.
[2]Larson, Don, *Guidelines for Barefoot Language Learning*, p. 93-94.

Five

Plans:
The Road
to Language Survival

You have made it this far. The in situ approach makes sense, but you have doubts; it seems a giant leap from theory to practice. This chapter focuses on the practical. It contains six complete lesson plans for situations you are likely to encounter. Each plan follows the daily learning cycle format explained in previous chapters.

Eventually you will design your own language program. But give yourself a break. Begin slowly. Use the following prepared lessons. By mastering them, you will gain basic tools in your target language, as well as learn a process that helps you continue learning. Before you begin, however, let's put the lessons into a broader perspective.

A LEARNING CYCLE APPROACH TO LESSON PLANNING

A good lesson plan is practical. It emphasizes common words and structures useful in many situations. If well chosen, your memorized passages will serve in actual conversation. A good lesson plan is also comprehensive. It provides options, more activities than you can handle in a single day, and possibilities to challenge you as your language skills improve.

The model lesson plans in this chapter prepare you for common experiences: eating out, buying in the marketplace and at a store, asking directions, handling money, defining words from spoken context. Each is a practical lesson, but each can also be used as the foundation for follow-up lessons after you have become more skilled or if you are already a more advanced learner. View your language lessons as grist for a spiraling cycle of learning. Though some situations remain generically the same (for example, dining out), the lesson should be designed to help you develop your ability to handle those situations in an increasingly complex manner.

A restaurant situation demonstrates the principle well. As a beginning learner you will be thrilled that you can order a dish, get your order, ask for a refill of tea, and pay the bill. As you become more advanced, you order a wider range of dishes, chat with restaurant staff, converse with luncheon companions. As you become proficient, you request particular seating, inquire about dishes prepared with a certain twist or not listed on the menu, converse at will in the target language, gracefully reject inferior food or service and compliment the excellent, and leave having enjoyed both food and conversation. Dining out becomes vastly more enjoyable for you as a proficient speaker than it was as a beginner. Yet, basic patterns underlie the dining out experience at all levels. Initially, you learn basic patterns. You build on them as your experience and ability grow.

The lessons offered in this chapter are not graded by ability. Some activities are for beginners; others for more advanced learners. Part of your preparation is to determine how best to adapt them to your needs. Don't plan to complete each lesson in a single session or day. Some will consume a week, even several weeks, depending upon how much time you devote and how many supplemental activities you do. Nor should you expect to finish any lesson, leaving it behind forever as you move on to the next. Rather, hone your skills at your current level. Return to the lesson, as you would to a favorite book, with more experience and insight. Master it again at a more advanced level.

The first sample lesson, a restaurant experience, contains passages at three levels to demonstrate the concept. The other five lessons present basic structures that you can adapt to your individual needs.

SAMPLE LESSON ONE
I'll Pass on the Pigsblood Soup, Thank You; or Finding Sustenance in a Local Cafe

1A. The Daily Learning Cycle—Novice Level

Decide. Your task is basic and immediate. You will sample a local cafe. You will order lunch and a cold drink, chat, then pay as you leave.

Prepare. You plan a dialogue with your mentor. You decide to order a local favorite, pork *adobo*, and a *calamansi*. By ordering something new, you not only expand your vocabulary, you increase your knowledge of local cuisine.

You also include two practical questions: how to ask for a refill and how to ask for your bill. The result? You create this passage (in your target language, not English):

"I'd like pork adobo with steamed rice. And a calamansi to drink."
[Later] "Excuse me, may I have another calamansi, please?"
[Later] "May we have the bill, please?"

Practice. Using the following guidelines, practice the passage.

- Initial listening drill. Your mentor recites the entire passage several times; she then repeats the passage sentence by sentence at normal speed until you begin to mouth the words as she recites.

- Backward build-up repetition drills. Beginning with the first sentence, your mentor drills you phrase by phrase (from the end forward) until you can say the entire sentence with ease. Then you do the second sentence, the third, and so on.

- Structure drills. Using the basic sentence patterns from your passage, develop drills that teach correct structure and that give you a few alternate menu items in case the cafe doesn't have what you order. Two short samples follow; your actual practice will be more extensive.

M: I'd like pork adobo, please.   *L: I'd like **pork adobo**, please.*
*M: **Chicken adobo***   *L: I'd like **chicken adobo**, please.*
*M: **Fish soup***   *L: I'd like **fish soup**, please.*
*M: **Steamed rice***   *L: I'd like **steamed rice**, please.*
                                      etc.

*M: Excuse me, may I have another **calamansi**?*
*L: Excuse me, may I have another **calamansi**?*
*M: **cup of coffee***
*L: Excuse me, may I have another **cup of coffee**?*

M: *fork*

L: *Excuse me, may I have another fork?*

M: *napkin*

L: *Excuse me, may I have another napkin?*
etc.

Role-play the anticipated cafe experience. Your mentor plays a waiter, and you work through several variations of the whole passage.

Wokabaot. Armed with your memorized passage and its variations, you're off to a local cafe where you try out the passage (and the cuisine). Order, eat, then return home to discuss the experience.

Evaluate and Practice. With your mentor, discuss the wokabaot and modify your passage based on the day's experience. As a result of your evaluation you do the following.

1. Add several questions likely to be asked by a waiter, recognizing that you need to understand what is said to you as well as to practice what you have to say.

2. Add an additional closing sentence, "Thank you, the meal was excellent!" (responding to your mentor's comment that one customarily expresses appreciation for the meal). This expands your original sentences into a true dialogue:

> **Waiter:** *Good afternoon, ladies.*
> **Learner:** *Good afternoon. May we have a table for two?*
> *[Later]* **W:** *Are you ready to order?*
> **L:** *Yes, I'd like pork adobo with steamed rice. And a calamansi to drink.*
> *[Later]* **L:** *Excuse me, may I have another calamansi?*
> **W:** *Certainly! May I bring you anything else?*
> **L:** *For me, just calamansi. But coffee for my friend.*
> *[Later]* **L:** *Thank you, the meal was excellent. May we have the bill, please?"*

3. Role-play for another fifteen minutes. This time you and your mentor alternate as waiter and customer, using the revised passage as the text. By day's end, the correct sentences are implanted both in your mind and on your tongue.

4. Ask your mentor to record the dialogue, first the full passage, then sentence by sentence. Have her pause long enough between sentences so you will be able to repeat each one after you hear it.

5. Agree to (1) listen to the tape at least ten times before tomorrow's session; (2) memorize the names of five local dishes (which she has given you); (3) practice them in self-directed drills; and (4) do at least one of the supplemental exercises listed below. Tomorrow's session will begin with more role plays of the restaurant passage.

1B. The Daily Learning Cycle—Intermediate Level

Decide. You have eaten at several local cafes. You can order a basic meal, but you can't really converse with your waiter. You realize also that most mealtime conversation is with your fellow diners; you need to practice "table talk." Finally, you want to say things about the future— so far, your restaurant dialogue has been in the present tense.

Prepare. With your mentor you expand your dialogue, anticipating the waiter's comments as well as planning your own. You end up with something like this (in the target language of course):

> **Waiter:** *Good afternoon, folks!*
> **Learner:** *Good afternoon, may we have a table for two?*
> *[Later]* **L:** *Do you have pork adobo? I'd like a large serving.*
> **W:** *I'm sorry. Normally we do, but we are just out!*
> **L:** *What is the house special today?*
> **W:** *We have an excellent arroz con pollo. [Pause] I'll return momentarily (for your order).*
> **W:** *Are you ready to order, ma'am?*
> **L:** *I'll have the arroz con pollo. To drink, calamansi.*
> *My friend would like paella valenciana and cafe.*
> *[Later]* **Mentor:** *How do you like the restaurant?*
> **L:** *It's attractive. Do you come here often?*
> **M:** *Frequently! And how do you like the music?*
> **L:** *It's good, but I like classical music better. What kind of music do you prefer?*
> *[You chat about music, having previously thought about the subject and prepared yourself for the topic.]*
> *[Later]* **L:** *Excuse me, I'd like another glass of calamansi, please.*
> **W:** *Certainly! Anything for you, ma'am?*
> *[Conversation continues]*
> *[Later]* **L:** *Thank you very much for the fine service.*
> *May we have the bill now, please?*

To practice speaking in future tense, you anticipate your likely route to the cafe and develop the following monologue to use on friends and friendly strangers en route:

> **L:** *We're on our way to Ni Song Cafe for lunch. I'm going to order pork adobo and calamansi. She's going to get something else. We'll be back after we eat.*

Practice. Using a range of drills, including listening drills, pattern drills and role plays, you practice the restaurant dialogue and the short passage explaining your trip.

Wokabaot. Armed with your memorized passage and its variations, you're off to a local cafe. You leave early enough to practice on the way. You stop briefly to chat with people along your normal route. Greet each one, exchange pleasantries, and try your new passage. Have lunch and then return home from the restaurant.

Evaluate and Practice. Examine your short dialogues and adjust them based on your experience. Develop drills on any questions you might have, and on misphrased or incorrect sentences, wrong word choices, incorrect verb endings, etc.

Practice your dialogue, tape record it, agree on homework, and set a time and place for your next session.

1C. The Daily Learning Cycle—Advanced Level

Decide. Eating out is no longer a chore. You can go to a restaurant, read the menu, ask about specials of the day, and get what you want. You use the restaurant situation as a way to practice special expressions, to identify and try out specialty foods, and/or to work on specific language structures with which you are having difficulty.

Prepare. You prepare drills on particular expressions which you believe you need to work on—at this level, probably relating to your dinner table conversation rather than specific language needed to address the restaurant staff. As an example, the conditional: "If he had told me earlier, I would have..."; "I might have considered it if she hadn't..."; "If you wait too long, we will have left."

Practice. Call upon your knowledge of drills to learn those expressions you have targeted for the session. Since you now have good command of basic structures, you emphasize free conversation rather than structured dialogues. You think of topics, then create and practice role plays based on only a sketch of the likely situation, rather than on memorized sentences. Ask your mentor to make notes on the wokabaot of any recurring problems with the targeted language structures, other recurring language errors, or errors in social behavior.

Wokabaot. Over the meal, and en route to and home from the cafe, you engage in free conversation, working your targeted expressions into the discussion as much as possible.

Evaluate and Practice. Discuss the experience with your mentor. If needed, design and practice drills to correct those errors identified by your mentor.

2. Supplemental Activities

For a different emphasis, try the following activities.

• Menu reading. In general, an in situ approach downplays reading as a beginning-level activity. Ordering in a restaurant is an exception. Ask your mentor to get a menu from the target restaurant and practice with it **before you go**. Have her read each item aloud as you look at the words. Repeat them after her. Read them yourself, item by item. Build substitution drills, using as your basic sentence, "May I have the [pork adobo]?" substituting each item on the menu for [pork adobo]. Finally, alternate roles as you simulate ordering from the menu. Ask your mentor to vary the drills to require choices or additional information. For example, "I'm sorry, sir, we're out of pork adobo; would you like *diniguan*?" "Which would you prefer, steamed or fried rice?"

• Food derivations. Develop drills which help you remember dishes by learning their ingredients.

> "Do you like [pork adobo]?"
> "Yes, I like it because it's made of [pork]!" "No, I don't like [pork] very much!" "Yes, I like the garlic flavor!" "No, I don't like the taste of garlic!"
> "Do you like [diniguan]?"
> "Yes, I like it because it's made of pig's blood!" "I don't like it very much; I'm not used to eating pig's blood." "Well, pig's blood certainly is different!"

• Cultural affirmations. Section 3, Cultural Notes, suggests cultural topics appropriate to a restaurant. Use them in affirmation drills: form your own hypotheses based on your observation, then let your mentor react to the hypotheses rather than describe behavior to you.

You might conclude, for instance, that "in this society, we should make a hissing sound to call a waiter to our table." Then, test your hypothesis by playing different roles with your mentor (e.g., a young male customer and older waiter, young male customer and young waitress, older female customer and older waiter, etc.) and by pretending to be in different restaurants. Your mentor's reaction in each situation will help you verify, refine, and reformulate your hypotheses.

3. Cultural Notes

Each learning activity generates questions about cultural differences and similarities, and strengthens your language-speaking ability as well. A restaurant visit offers an excellent opportunity to sharpen your observational skills. As you eat, exercise your eyes and ears, and ask your mentor such questions as these:

How do I get a waiter's attention? With a wave, a hand or finger motion, a hissing sound, a clucking noise, some other action? Is it the same for a waitress?

How do I address a waiter? A waitress? Do I use certain terms or phrases, intonation or tone changes?

How do I order? Does one member of the party order for all or do people order individually? Does everyone order the same dish? If so, how does the group reach its decision? (Careful on this one: in some societies it is done so subtly you may miss it the first three hundred times!) Who orders first?

What do we talk about? Is there a preferred "table talk"? What topics are inappropriate as table conversation?

Are some dishes appropriate for certain meals, but not others? If, for example, everyone eats eggs and rice for breakfast, chances are that **if** you can get a cafe to serve you toast and juice, you will pay dearly for it. Flow with custom—you will save money and time.

How do I eat? Which foods are finger foods? Which are eaten with utensils? Are certain foods customarily eaten in a certain order? For example, coffee is often considered an after-dinner drink. You may have difficulty ordering it with your meal or buying it by itself ("going out for a cup of coffee").

How do I decline? What is an appropriate response if I prefer not to eat a certain dish? Can I refuse a proffered food? If so, how? Am I expected to eat or drink food given to me? How much of it?

How do I pay? Is a certain member of the party expected to pay? Who? Where do I pay? Is tipping expected? How much? To whom?

4. Spin-off Activities

Each learning cycle activity should spawn ideas for follow-up ventures that can broaden your language base. Consider these activities to supplement a restaurant excursion.

- Marketplace visit. Visit the marketplace to learn about foods you are unfamiliar with and find out how they are used.

- Food preparation. Learn to prepare local dishes. Learn the ingredients, find out where to buy them. Write down the recipe; using it is good practice in following directions. (It is also good survival planning. Begin with simple dishes that you like and can make easily at home.)

- Restaurant comparison. Become an unofficial food critic. Visit several restaurants, order the same dish in each, and sharpen your comparative senses. Expand your knowledge of local dishes: return to the same restaurant, each time ordering a different item.

- Family meals. Eat with a family whenever you have the opportunity. What are the staples in the local diet? How are they prepared? What beverages commonly come with a home meal? Who eats together? Who eats separately? Where do people eat? What do people talk about while they eat? What are the expected table manners? Are certain foods prepared only for special occasions? What roles do different sexes perform in food preparation, serving, conversation, cleanup, etc.?

- Formal meals. Look for different patterns when you attend a formal dinner, banquet, or feast. Are special dishes featured that are not normally served? Do topics of conversation differ? What rituals accompany the eating—speeches, introductions, prayers, toasts, etc?

5. Mini-bibliography

Food offers potential for greatly expanding your vocabulary. The language of eating is extensive. Each book in the *Berlitz* [...] *for Travellers* series offers an extensive restaurant vocabulary. A similar book, the *American Express International Traveler's Pocket* [...] *Dictionary and Phrase Book*, also offers useful phrases. Both series are language-specific, but the English equivalents are useful for ideas in any language. Clark's short book, *Potluck*, explores American foods, but the exercises following each introductory session offer examples for food-related discussion in any language.

SAMPLE LESSON TWO
Excuse Me, Sir, How Did I Get from There to Here? or How to Find Your Way Home before Dark

1. The Daily Learning Cycle

Decide. You are about to venture out for a bit of sightseeing. You want to find your destinations and return home safely. Today's task: work on learning to ask and follow directions.

Prepare. Your mentor suggests a widely known landmark as a reference point. Our Lady of Guadalupe Cathedral fits the bill; it's near la Plaza de Reforma and el Museo de las Artes Modernas, your main destinations. From the cathedral you can find the museum and plaza easily, your mentor assures you. You plan to go by bus, so you consult the map and consider several routes. You decide to start from the corner of 16 de Septiembre and Miguel Hidalgo streets (so you know how to get to the cathedral **before you ask**). You prepare the following passage (in the target language):

> *A: Excuse me, ma'am, which bus goes to Our Lady of Guadalupe?*
> *B: The one marked Las Palmas, young lady! You can catch it over there!*
> *A: [On boarding] What's the fare to Our Lady of Guadalupe?*
> *B: Five hundred pesos, miss! [Takes money; makes change.]*
> *A: I'm new here. Can you tell me when to get off to go to Our Lady of Guadalupe?*
> *B: Certainly, miss!*
> *A: [After getting off the bus] Excuse me, ma'am, can you help me? How do I get to la Plaza de Reforma?*
> *B: Acrossthestreet,downtheblock,turnrightandthereyou'llbe!*
> *A: I'm sorry, ma'am. I'm just learning Spanish. Would you speak more slowly please.*
> *B: Go across the street. Walk that way down the block. Turn right at la Calle del Infierno. You'll come right to it.*
> *A: Thanks for your help. I'll be going now!*

Practice. Use the following exercises to learn the passage and related structures and vocabulary.

- A listening drill. Your mentor recites the full passage several times, then sentence by sentence at normal speed. Continue to listen until you can mouth the words as he recites.

- Backward build-up repetition drills. Drill until you can say each sentence completely and correctly. Your mentor builds backwards from a sentence fragment to the entire sentence. Next, master the response in the same manner. Practice the question, then the response, changing roles with your mentor. Tackle the second question, its response, etc., until you have mastered the entire passage.

- Follow-up substitution drills. Expand your range of questions and possible responses as in the following examples. Again, ask your mentor to be sure that the drills employ realistic language, that no sentences sound strange in the target language.

M: What is the fare to Our Lady ...?
  L: What is the fare to Our Lady ... ?

M: La Plaza ...	*L: What is the fare to **La Plaza** ...?*
M: El Museo ...	*L: What is the fare to **El Museo**...?*

M: Turn right at la Calle del Infierno.
  *L: **Turn right** at la Calle del Infierno.*

M: Turn left	*L: **Turn left** at la Calle del Infierno.*
M: Go straight	*L: **Go straight** at la Calle del Infierno.*
M: Go back	*L: **Go back** at la Calle del Infierno.* etc.

M: Turn right at the next block.
  *L: Turn right at the **next** block.*

M: second	*L: Turn right at the **second** block.*
M: last	*L: Turn right at the **last** block.* etc.

Vary your practice with potential destinations (including how to get back to your starting point), types of transportation, and directions.

Destinations: the post office, airport, train station, bus stop, bathroom, public telephone, corner of 16 de Septiembre and Miguel Hidalgo streets, a particular bank, restaurant, hotel.

Transportation: bus, taxi, train, metro (subway).

Directions: left, right; straight ahead; forward, back; next, last; east, west, north, south.

- Role plays. Conclude the session with role plays, exchanging roles so that you learn both to question and to respond.

Wokabaot. Today you are armed with more than your memorized passage and its variations. With your lunch, a map, walking shoes, and a pocketful of change for bus fare, you chat briefly with friends along your normal walking route, exchange pleasantries and explain today's excursion: "Hi, I'm going museum-hopping. First I'll go to the corner of 16 de Septiembre and Miguel Hidalgo. I'll ask a stranger where to catch a bus to Our Lady of Guadalupe. I'll take the correct bus, get off at the cathedral, then ask another stranger...."

Then try out the passage (using each component at its appropriate place), tour the church, plaza, museum, etc., each time asking directions to the next location from another stranger. Eventually, wend your way home, stopping en route to chat with friends and summarize today's excursion. "Hi, I've been to.... I saw the cathedral. Then I went to the plaza...."

Evaluate and Practice. Discuss the excursion with your mentor. Modify the passage, add responses you hadn't anticipated and questions you didn't know how to ask. As follow-up, try the following:

1. Conduct pattern drills to memorize the revised passage.

2. Role-play events from the excursion. Again, exchange roles and practice both asking and answering questions.

3. Ask your mentor to record the dialogue, including the full passage, as well as sentence-by-sentence components. Leave enough space so you can repeat each sentence after you have heard it on the tape.

4. Agree to study the taped passage and do one supplemental activity before your next session.

5. Agree on general objectives for the next session.

2. Supplemental Activities

The following activities will provide additional practice.

- Physical Response Drill. This drill requires you to demonstrate that you understand directions. Respond with actions, rather than spoken answers.

  M: Go three steps and turn left.
    L: [Takes three steps and then turns left.]
  M: Walk three steps and turn **right**.
    L: [Completes task.]
  M: Walk **forward** nine steps and turn **right**.
    L: [Does so.]
  etc.

  Note: You can expand this exercise to include additional speaking practice. As you follow each instruction, explain your actions (in the target language). For example, "I am taking three steps; now I am turning left" or "I took three steps and turned left."

- Confirmation drill. You learned how to ask and give directions in earlier practice. Turn the situation around; practice phrases so that strangers can confirm directions for you (rather than give them to you).

L: *I'm going to Our Lady of Guadalupe. To get there I go across the street, down the block, and turn right at la Calle del Infierno. Is that correct?*
M: *[Confirms or modifies]*
　L: *I'm going to la Plaza de Reforma. To get there I go ....*
　Is that correct?
M: *[Confirms or modifies]*

- Questioning exercise. You can create practice opportunities on your wokabaot if every two or three blocks you ask someone else for directions. Stop someone, ask her how to get to [la Plaza de Reforma]. As soon as she is out of sight, stop someone else and ask him.

- Map Walking. Find a detailed street map of the city. Mark those locations you want to visit: the post office, la Plaza de Reforma, the corner of 16 de Septiembre and Hidalgo, your house, etc. Travel by fingertip from place to place on your map. Describe your trip as you go.

  To practice comprehension, as your mentor gives directions, trace the route on the map with your fingers. You can progress from simple directions such as "turn right" to more complicated forms such as "follow Highway 31 for about six kilometers past the tenth intersection until you reach the primary school at the corner of ..., then...."

  Practice giving directions by directing your mentor or study partner from one spot on the map to another.

  Before you plan a specific journey, use a map exercise to learn the proposed route and an alternative. Practice traveling to the proposed destination and home again.

- Model building. Need something more concrete than a map? Construct a model village. Make it simple: sticks, stones, bottles, tin cans. Or be more creative: use cartons and boxes; draw in doors, windows, and store names. Better yet, go whole hog, and build a scale model city using natural materials. A model gives more visual impact to your direction-giving practice.

3. Cultural Notes

Different cultures ask for and give information in different ways. Look and listen as you ask directions.

What gestures do people use to show direction? Do they point with certain fingers, their hands or bodies, their lips?

Are directions explicit or imprecise?

What comparative, but imprecise directional words are used? Listen for words analogous to "far" or "far away" or "a long way away," which, though imprecise, indicate comparative distance.

Be alert for different conceptions of distance: "It's just down the road" might mean, for instance, an hour's walk (if you're in shape). Further, you may find that speakers offer what they think you *want* to hear. Have your mentor help you phrase your questions to minimize this problem.

What etiquette governs hailing, boarding, and riding on public transportation? Do taxis stop only at certain points? Does one hail a taxi or bus with a wave, motion, sound, stance? What rules govern waiting for and boarding a taxi, bus, subway, or train?

4. Spin-off Activities

As follow-up to your initial wokabaot, try the following activities.

- An all-day excursion. Plan major excursions well in advance, using a learning cycle session or sessions to prepare for the entire trip. Simulate the excursion with your mentor; walk your daily route and ask your friends to suggest sights, activities, shopping hints for your excursion. Let them help you envision the location and possible activities. View your excursion as an extended wokabaot, filling a day or a weekend.

- Destination-specific dialogues. Develop passages to use at specific places on your wokabaot, for example, buying stamps at the post office, changing traveler's checks at the bank, buying an airplane or bus ticket, eating lunch.

- Cultural discussion dialogues. Once you are beyond minimum survival skill, develop dialogues that delve into the cultural meaning of institutions or locations you have visited, for instance, the role of the church in modern society; the development and functions of the plaza concept; public transportation facilities in the city.

5. Mini-bibliography

Each book in the *Berlitz* [...] *for Travellers* series provides numerous examples of direction giving and locations one might visit. See Jerald and Clark's *Experiential Language Teaching Techniques* (pp. 24-41) for map, directions, car, and bus/metro exercises. Fantini's *Beyond the Language Classroom* (pp. 43-44) presents an exercise using the map of a country (rather than a city street map).

SAMPLE LESSON THREE
Speaking the Language of High Finance; or How to Trade Paper for Hard Cash

1. The Daily Learning Cycle

Decide. Your first shot at exchanging a traveler's check came at the airport the afternoon you arrived. It was simple, really. You approached the booth, pushed across a traveler's check, mumbled and pointed. The guy in the booth filled out some forms, figured for a few moments, then pushed a pile of money at you. You didn't count it. The bills were different colors and sizes; you didn't know one from the other. You want to try again (having run out of money), but with more finesse.

Prepare. Overcoming the urge to deal with the guy who hangs out in the alleyway and hisses, "Psssst, Americano!" as you walk by, you have decided to trade at a local bank. Develop (in the target language) the following:

> *A: Good morning! May I change a $50 traveler's check?*
> *B: Yes, sir. May I see your identification—a passport?*
> *[Pause to fill out forms] Your local address, sir?*
> *A: It's 32 Calle Turista, Apartamento 19. I would like most of it in [2,000 peso] bills. May I also have some change for bus rides?*
> *B: Here you are, sir. Thank you!*
> *A: And thank you.*

Practice. Use the following types of exercises to learn the passage and related structure and vocabulary.

- A simple listening drill. Your mentor recites the passage several times. She then repeats it sentence by sentence at normal speed until you can mouth the words as she recites.

- Background build-up repetition drills. Beginning with the first sentence, drill until you can say each sentence completely and correctly. Learn the response, the second sentence and its response, the third, etc. Change roles with your mentor and master both question and response.

- Substitution drills. Develop and practice questions and responses to learn currency denominations.

  > *M: May I change this **traveler's check**?*
  > *L: May I change this **traveler's check**?*
  > *M: **10,000 peso note***
  > *L: May I change this **10,000 peso note**?*

M: 5,000 peso note
  *L: May I change this **5,000 peso note**?*
M: 2,000 peso note
  *L: May I change this **2,000 peso note**?*
M: Do you have some identification?
  L: Do you have some identification?

*M: **change for this bill**?*
  *L: Do you have **change for this bill**?*
*M: **a smaller note**?*
  *L: Do you have **a smaller note**?*
*M: **a 20-peso coin**?*
  *L: Do you have **a 20-peso coin**?*
etc.

- Money identification exercise. Use this exercise to learn the country's currency (see supplemental activities below).

- Role play. With your mentor, role-play the anticipated exchange. Your mentor plays the teller, and you practice several variations. Anticipate your route to the bank and role-play what you will say to the friends you meet en route (see the following for suggestions).

Wokabaot. Today you are armed with your memorized passage, your traveler's checks, and your passport. Stop and chat with friends but hedge a bit on your destination. What with the general belief that all Americans are rich, it makes little sense to broadcast that you will have extra cash in your pockets. Rather, talk about a secondary objective such as buying stamps and post cards.

Try your passage at a neighborhood bank, spend a few pesos at the post office, buy post cards, and return home. En route home, chat with friends, describe today's excursion, and show them the stamps and postcards you bought.

Evaluate and Practice. Discuss the wokabaot with your mentor, modify the passage, adding responses you hadn't planned and questions you didn't ask. Then try the following:

1. Work through pattern drills to master the new sentences.

2. Role-play situations from the excursion. Practice both questioning and answering.

3. Have your mentor record the dialogue, first the full passage and then sentence by sentence. Have her include pauses so you will be able to repeat each sentence individually.

4. Agree on follow-up for the next session, and agree to study the

cassette and practice at least two counting exercises from the supplemental activities below.

    5. Decide the general emphasis of the next session.

2. Supplemental Activities

    Successful money exchange rests on recognizing basic numbers as well as local currency. The following activities, several of which you can do by yourself, build both skills.

    Basic counting. Before you can comfortably handle local currency, you need a firm grasp of basic numbers. Your goal should be to internalize numbers in the target language without translating from English. Try these rapid-response exercises.

- Finger drills. Your fingers will take you from one to ten. Learn to count forward and backward; add your toes to master one to twenty. Vary the numbers; randomly put up nine, four, seven fingers, etc. Get someone to practice with you (a neighborhood kid, for example).

- Gaming drills. Any game with dice, dominoes, numbered cards, or moves on a board can help you learn numbers. For example, roll a pair of dice (then two pair for higher numbers) and see how quickly you can respond in the target language with the correct number. If you are daring, join a friendly crap game; you will learn numbers as well as how to handle (and lose) local currency.

- Calendar drills. Use your calendar to learn the numbers from one through thirty-one. Point at random to, or throw darts at, dates on your calendar. Learn to recite them in the target language without translating.

- Physical response drills. Have your mentor ask you: "Clap [ten] times," "Hop [three] times," "Go get us [two] cold beers," etc. Demonstrate your understanding by carrying out the appropriate action.

- Cuisenaire rods. If you had appropriate foresight, you liberated your little sister's Cuisenaire rods before you left home. (They are a set of small wooden blocks in ten different lengths—"one" represented by a cube; "two" the length of two cubes; "three," three; etc. Each length is a different color. They provide excellent practice in math and numbers, as well as colors.) If you can't find them locally, ask a U.S. friend to mail you some. The purchased ones are a good buy because they include a booklet of exercises. If you can't beg or borrow some, make your own.

Money exchange. You can develop any number of exercises and simulations to practice handling the local currency, as well as to work on the adding and subtracting skills you need to buy merchandise and receive change. Whenever possible, use real money for your practice; get $50 worth in a variety of denominations and practice regularly with them. You should work on the following skills.

- Identifying. Separate different bills and coins into piles, then point out the value of each. Have your mentor point to different piles, which you identify. Have your mentor mix the bills, hold them poker-style in her hand, and ask you to pick different bills.

- Adding and subtracting. Simply add (and subtract) bills (e.g., un mil pesos + un mil pesos = dos mil pesos; dos mil pesos + un mil pesos = tres mil pesos), using your bills in as many combinations as you can.

- Buying and selling. Simulate marketplace buying. Pretend that a set of items (e.g., rocks, candy bars, mango pits) are merchandise. Ask the price, have your mentor sell you one, then count out the proper amount. Do it in reverse: have your mentor pay too much; count out the proper change. Make it more challenging: practice identifying objects as well as currency, for example, different fruit (three papaya, two mangoes, twenty-one lemons) or household items (nine plates, four chairs, one table).

Money value. You will gradually become aware of the local currency's purchasing power—the cost of bread, rice, Coca-Cola Classic, and stamps become second nature. To hasten your ability to think in terms of local purchasing value rather than translation from the dollar, try the following.

- Pricing. Place several objects on a table, along with an assortment of coins and bills. Elicit the expression, "How much?" or "How much does it cost?" from your mentor. Learn the value of each item by moving the appropriate amount of money next to each. Vary the exercise by grouping items (four mangoes, two mangoes and two papayas, a dozen airmail stamps, a pair of sandals and a hat).

- Comparative pricing. Assemble a collection of items and identify their comparative values—a hammer costs more than a mango but less than a saw; a pencil costs less than a mango but more than a banana.

- Budgeting. Develop a monthly budget in the local currency. Lay out categories of expenses—rent, transportation, school fees, food, entertainment. Estimate and track expenses in the local currency **and** percent of monthly income. To expand your thinking beyond small items, develop a wish list of items and express them as a percentage of your monthly income in local currency rather than dollars—an expensive stereo, motorcycle, car, air fare to your home in the U.S., a weekend at a local five-star hotel.

3. Cultural Notes

Chances are that banking etiquette will be different from what you are used to. Ask yourself and your mentor questions like these.

Do banking transactions require that you wait in different lines? If there are lines, do people regularly cut in? If so, who?

Are transactions handled sequentially? Do I give my traveler's check to one clerk, then move to a different line to receive the money from another?

Are customers helped other than in a first-come, first-served basis? For instance, must I get a number, then wait until that number has been called before being helped?

Are foreign currency transactions handled by a special clerk or in a separate location in the bank?

Is there a transaction fee? (Probably! Many banks charge a small fee to convert money. You are not being discriminated against; it's a charge everyone pays).

What do I do with the paperwork? (You will get receipts of your transactions. Keep them. You may need to show customs you have abided by currency transaction laws.)

When we are first overseas, many of us feel vulnerable in the money exchange game, fearful that people are taking advantage of us. Set high priority on learning the currency to overcome those first negative feelings. Also, keep in mind two basic money exchange principles. First, rates change, generally daily. Banks post current rates; you can easily find out the going rate. Second, rates differ. Rates for conversion **from** dollars into local currency are different from conversion **into** dollars from local currency. Banks pay different rates for traveler's checks and actual greenbacks. Businesses will exchange traveler's checks and currency at different rates from those given by banks.

Note: if currency exchange worries you, buy a currency calculator (a small electronic calculator that figures the exchange for you based on the day's exchange rate).

4. Spin-off Activities

Metric conversion practice. Most likely your purchase of foodstuffs will involve not only currency conversion, but also metric measurement. You should begin to visualize metric measures in terms of quantity, rather than their equivalents in pounds, inches, or quarts. Also, many countries use their own measures as well—a certain-sized bowl or container, for instance. To develop drills that help you visualize metric and local measurements, you will need the following:

- Measures for dry goods: a kilo of rice, beans or wheat; containers that hold exactly 500, 250, 100 grams, and/or common local sizes,

- Measures for liquids: containers for a decaliter of water, a liter, 500 centiliters, and/or common local sizes,

- An image of distance: a meter stick will help you think in centimeters rather than inches. For travel distances, use a map of the country to learn kilometers between major important points. Develop distance-recognition drills (see the map walking exercise in sample lesson 2) that help you think in kilometers rather than miles.

Time as value comparisons. Your earlier practice taught you to think of local currency in terms of how much you can buy. For an enlightening exercise, view currency in terms of the hours people work to purchase various items. With your mentor's help, compile a list of approximate local wage rates. Calculate how many hours people in different occupations must work to buy various items: an imported radio, a car, a week's worth of rice. If you earn an American dollar salary, compare your earnings to your host country coworkers. This exercise should lead to interesting (and soul-searching) discussions with friends and coworkers on being an expatriate employee.

5. Mini-bibliography

For exercises on numbers and basic mathematics, see the activity cards included with Kunz's *Modern Mathematics Made Meaningful* (written for use with cuisenaire rods, it is useful for a variety of exercises). Books in the *Berlitz [...] for Travellers* series contain useful phrases for banking and shopping, numbers, and metric conversion.

SAMPLE LESSON FOUR
Yes, Ma'am, I'd Like Six of Those Green Things!
or How to Shop Like a Native

1. The Daily Learning Cycle

Decide. Haggling is the tourist's traditional delight, a game (or horror, depending on your background and inclination). For those living abroad, however, it's an essential part of daily life. True, anyone can bargain, but you want to move beyond pointing, grunts, three-word target-language monologues, broken English, and wild gestures. You want to shop with some semblance of grace and aplomb, to sharpen your shopping skills, as well as learn about available foods.

Prepare. Your mentor suggests you look for two fruits you have not tasted, *atis* and *siniguwelas*. Further, he advises, you won't find fresh bread in the marketplace; you must shop at one of the small bakeries in the area. As a result, together you create two short passages for today's *wokabaot* that go something like this:

> *A: Good morning, how much are the atis?*
> *B: Only 200 pesos for six.*
> *A: That's very expensive. Will you sell them for 50 pesos?*
> *B: Oh, no sir! That is not possible.*
> *A: How about 75 pesos?*
> *B: I cannot, sir. But for 175 pesos it would be possible.*
> *A: They look delicious. I'll give you 100 pesos.*
> *[Bargaining continues] And how much are these papayas?*
> *B: For you, sir, only 150 pesos!*
> *A: That seems too high. Do you have a better price?*
> *[An hour later, after having purchased two small papayas, four atis, and a half-dozen siniguwelas, you plod into a bakery for bread—and much needed rest.]*
> *A: Good morning, what is this? [pointing] And this?*
> *B: I'll take ten rolls, and one loaf of that, please.*
> *A: How much will that be?*
> *B: Eighty-five pesos, sir.*
> *A: Here you go. Thank you.*
> *B: And thank you, sir.*

Practice. Using the following, practice each passage until you can say it fluently from memory. Then work on related structures and vocabulary.

- A listening drill. Your mentor recites the first passage several times. He then recites each sentence at normal speed until you can mouth the words as he talks.

- Backward build-up repetition drills. Beginning with the first sentence, drill until you can say each sentence completely and correctly, continuing until you have memorized the entire dialogue. Play both roles so you can practice both questioning and responding.

- Substitution drills. Develop drills to practice different potential purchases. Several samples follow:

  M: How much are these papayas?
     L: How much are these papayas?

M: atis?	*L: How much are these atis?*
M: siniguwelas?	*L: How much are these siniguwelas?*
M: isda?	*L: How much are these isda? etc.*

  M: That's very expensive. Will you sell it for 50 pesos?
     L: That's very expensive. Will you sell it for 50 pesos?

  | *M: 100?* | *L: ... Will you sell it for 100 pesos?* |
  | *M: 150?* | *L: ... Will you sell it for 150 pesos? etc.* |

  M: That's very expensive. Will you sell 8 for 200 pesos?
     L: That's very expensive. Will you sell 8 for 200 pesos?

  | *M: 6?* | *L: ... Will you sell 6 for 200 pesos?* |
  | *M: 5?* | *L: ... Will you sell 5 for 200 pesos? etc.* |

- Money exchange drills. Review the money exchange exercises (sample lesson 3). Drill using the currency you might use at the market.

- Role play. With your mentor, role-play marketplace bargaining, practicing each item you expect to buy. Exchange roles so you learn both to question and to respond. Because buying fresh fruit differs from buying bread, your role plays account for the different atmospheres and buying strategies. Anticipate your route to the marketplace and role-play short conversations with the friends you might see en route and on returning home.

Wokabaot. Today's wokabaot requires two special tools of the trade: plenty of small change and your favorite shopping bag or basket. (Unless you are an excellent juggler or have a small appetite, you will need your own container for your purchases. It's usually "bring your own bag" in the marketplace.) Duly outfitted, take off to greet friends en route, exchange pleasantries, and explain this morning's wokabaot.

Wander through the market, eavesdrop on exchanges between experienced shoppers and vendors, find the appropriate stalls, and, item by item, buy your fruit. Take your time, make small talk, and simply absorb the atmosphere.

Stop at a bakery, try your second passage, and buy bread. Eventually trudge back to your starting location, chat briefly with some of your regulars along the way, discuss your trip, and show them today's purchases. When you arrive home hot, sweaty, and tired, collapse on the settee, down three cold drinks, and, after discarding thoughts of calling it a day, move on to evaluation.

Evaluate and Practice. Discuss the experience with your mentor, modify the basic passage, adding responses you hadn't planned, and questions you didn't know how to ask. Then work through these familiar steps.

1. Develop and practice pattern drills to implant the revised sentence structures in your mind.

2. Role-play several vendor-buyer exchanges, trying both roles to practice both questioning and answering.

3. Ask your mentor to record the revised dialogue, both the full passage and sentence-by-sentence components.

4. Agree to study the cassette, bring a list of at least three things you need to buy, and then try one of the supplemental activities before the next session.

2. Supplemental Activities

The following exercises will give you additional shopping practice.

Comparative buying. Purchase different goods with different buying strategies, language, and demeanor. Work out with your mentor strategies for buying the following:

- Clothing. Try purchasing footwear, shirts or blouses, dresses or trousers, a hat. Learn local equivalents to such questions as, "May I try it on?" "I'd like a pair of...." "Do you have anything less expensive?" "Do you have a larger (smaller) size?" "Do you have something darker (lighter)?" "Do you have it in brown (blue)?"
- Toiletries. "Where can I find shaving cream (tampons, soap, toothpaste)?"
- Postal and writing supplies. "Do you have envelopes (pens, writing paper, post cards)?"
- Services. These include getting a haircut, having clothes tailor-

made, getting your car fixed or watch repaired. "Will you cut my hair (fix my watch, make me a shirt)?" "The problem is that my watch won't (start, run, keep time)."

Scavenger hunt. List ten or fifteen common items you might need, then look for them in the central market. Agree to buy no more than two from any given vendor or store. Include things new to you (e.g., food you have not tasted, implements you have never used—a coconut scraper, for example) and other familiar things you might need (a comb or toothbrush, wrapping paper, twine, an elementary school textbook, camera battery). Add to your list some local food or drink available only from certain types of vendors (and when you find it, take a break and enjoy it). Before you start, work up with your mentor useful questions such as, "Where can I find ...?" "Do you know who sells ...?"

Grab-bag purchase. Go to the marketplace, buy an inexpensive implement that is new to you, find out its use, and have your mentor teach you (or direct you to someone who can teach you) how to use it. Before you go, practice some likely questions: "What do people use this for?" "What is this item called?" "How do we use this properly?" "How is this made?" "Did you make this yourself?"

3. Cultural Notes

Bargaining is often an accepted, expected part of shopping in many parts of Africa [as it is in other parts of the world]. As an American, you are thought to be rich by many of the people from whom you will be buying and this preconception of theirs will often affect the bargaining procedure, prices asked, and willingness to come down in price. As with any other social exchanges, there are accepted polite procedures and structures for bargaining which are both socially important and financially profitable to master.
—*An Expanded Collection of Language Informant Techniques*, Gary Engelberg, 1975 (p. 23).

Different rules govern buying in different situations. Think about the difference in going to a U.S. car dealer, a garage sale, or Safeway. You use different language and different approaches in the different situations. Imagine, if you will, trying to convince the produce manager at Safeway to sell strawberries for 60¢ a pound instead of $1.89 as posted! Or the effectiveness of kicking the tires of a new Mercedes, calling it a "gawdawful piece of junk," and the salesman "a lying scoundrel." Ask yourself and your mentor questions like the following:

What items does one bargain for? What items sell for a fixed price?

If a fixed price, which stores or vendors tend to offer the best bargains?

Are there different situations under which one can (or cannot) bargain for the same item? Are there certain stores? Sections of the city? Times of day in which bargaining rules differ?

What strategies are commonly used to bargain? Does one depre- cate an item or the seller, praise the item and/or the seller, emphasize one's inability to pay the asking price, or one's needs, e.g., the demands of your sick infant? Does one compare the vendor's price to prices elsewhere? try to get a lower asking price? more items for the same price? both?

What relationships exist between vendor and buyer? How does that vary by product? (In some Filipino markets, for instance, one can establish a *suki* relationship with some market vendors: the buyer settles in to buying regularly from a particular vendor who in turn guarantees a certain allotment or quality of item for the buyer. The relationship requires trust and a different purchasing etiquette.)

4. Spin-off Activities

Marketplace awareness. View the marketplace from the vendor's perspective. Spend time (during the slow part of the day) chatting with vendors. Where do they get their goods? When do they come to work, and from how far away? How much profit do they earn on their sales? (Ask indirectly, e.g., how much fifty papayas would cost them, then figure it out yourself.)

We once spent a sobering afternoon in the Acapulco marketplace chatting with vendors. We taught them English phrases they said they needed to deal effectively with American tourists: "Please don't throw my [merchandise] on the ground!" "Please give the item back if you don't want to buy it!" "Please don't stand on my [merchandise]!"

Cooking class. With your mentor, list ingredients for a common local dish. Buy each item in the market, and (under the supervision of someone who knows how to cook the dish) cook up a pot. Then serve lunch to your friends.

Take your cooking expert with you to the market. He can demon- strate (in the target language) the finer points of shopping: how to get a good cut of meat from a hanging side of beef, how to detect bruises on *singkamas*, how to judge the age and quality of rice.

Let a local cook supervise your cooking and teach you the basics: How hot is a good fire (and how do you judge the temperature of flame or coals)? What are the proper pans and pots for each dish? (Can you believe that some Americans cook rice in the same pot they use for cooking other foods?) What are the optimum cooking times, proper seasoning and sauces? Finally, prepare the same dish several times. You will need more than one try to accomplish an acceptable rendition, both culinary and linguistic. No use butchering another dish until your first one meets minimal local standards.

5. Mini-bibliography

Begin with your copy of the *Berlitz [...] for Travellers*. The sections on shopping and eating offer a wealth of ideas. See also Fantini, *Beyond the Language Classroom* (pp. 40-42), for several food-related exercises and Jerald and Clark's *Experiential Language Teaching Techniques* (pp. 46-53) for variations on the scavenger hunt suggestion.

SAMPLE LESSON FIVE
Quickly, Sir, What Do You Have for Diarrhea?
or How to Plan for Sudden Distress

1. The Daily Learning Cycle

Decide. Traveling abroad has downers as well as uppers. So far you may have been lucky, but aches and pains will come. Make sure your medical kit has the basics: something for indigestion, diarrhea, colds, sunburn, cuts and scrapes, a sore throat, headache, and insect bites. Your task is to visit a pharmacy, meet the pharmacist (or chemist), stock up on supplies, and develop your linguistic ability to cope with illness and injury.

Prepare. As you plan your excursion, the problem of translation becomes apparent. You may be unable to find Band-Aids, not realizing that locally people use *plasters*. Try to think in terms of use (something to cover up cuts and scrapes) rather than product names. To get started, you develop something similar to the following dialogue (in the target language).

> *A: Good afternoon. I need something for diarrhea!*
> *B: Yes, sir! We have several products. How about [...]!*
> *A: Which do you recommend?*
> *[Lengthy explanation expressing virtues of each product, spoken rapidly, and shot full of medical jargon.]*
> *A: Thank you, sir. I'll buy a bottle of this one.*
> *B: Will there be anything else?*
> *A: Yes, what do you have for sunburn ... and cuts and scrapes... and indigestion ... and....*
> *B: Sacre bleu, monsieur ... are you opening a hospital?*
> *(or some similar response, followed by laughter all around, and the start of a new friendship)*

Practice. Using the following, practice the dialogue until you can say each sentence fluently from memory. Then work on new or troublesome structures and vocabulary.

- A listening drill. Your mentor recites the entire passage several times. She then recites the passage sentence by sentence at normal speed until you can mouth the words as she recites.

- Backward build-up repetition drills. Beginning with the first sentence, drill until you can say each sentence completely and correctly. Begin with the last piece of the sentence and build forward to the entire sentence. Master each sentence, continuing until you finish. Change roles so you practice questioning and responding.

- Structure drill. Develop and practice drills on different purchases.

  M: I need something for diarrhea.
     *L: I need something for **diarrhea**.*

M: sunburn	*L: I need something for **sunburn**.*
M: a cut	*L: I need something for **a cut**.*
M: indigestion	*L: I need something for **indigestion**.*
M: a sore throat	*L: I need something for **a sore throat**.*
	etc.

- Role play. Try role-playing anticipated purchases. Your mentor plays the pharmacist as you make different purchases. Your role plays use heavy doses of charades, so practice the gestures needed to convey a variety of presumed illnesses. Anticipate your route to the pharmacy and role-play brief exchanges with friends you will visit en route.

Wokabaot. With little ado, you are off to the shopping area to find a friendly (and patient) druggist. Greet friends along the route, exchange pleasantries, and explain your outing. Chat with one druggist and buy a couple of items. Visit one or two other pharmacies, meet several druggists, and buy all your needed items. In the process you will probably learn of several popular products you didn't know existed.

On the way home, chat with friends and show off (some of) your day's purchases. Ignore their jibes that you must be a hypochondriac and move on to evaluation of your wokabaot.

Evaluate and Practice. Discuss the excursion with your mentor, modify the passage, and add responses you hadn't planned and questions you didn't know how to ask.

1. Practice drills of the revised passage.

2. Role-play selected exchanges from the wokabaot. Again, exchange roles so that you can improve both your questioning and answering skills.

3. Have your mentor record the revised dialogue, both the full passage and sentence by sentence, leaving enough space for you to repeat each sentence individually.

4. Agree on follow-up activities to be completed before the next session. Agree to memorize the passage from the tape and plan a word guess exercise (see below).

5. Decide the major objectives for the next session.

2. Supplemental Activities

Try the following for additional practice.

Word Guess. Write a number of words for illnesses, physical problems, injuries, medicines, and toiletries on separate scraps of paper (in the target language). Place them in a bowl. With your mentor or partner, take turns selecting words at random. Define them aloud (in the target language). Each of you should try to define the words precisely enough for the other to be able to identify them quickly and easily.

Doctor/patient. Take turns being doctor and patient. As patient, pretend you have an illness or symptom. Describe the symptom clearly enough for your "doctor" to identify it and suggest an appropriate remedy. As doctor, diagnose the problem and explain appropriate treatment. If you are an advanced speaker, you can emphasize the cultural differences in medical care by discussing local remedies.

First aid practice. Organize a first aid course, requesting local medical people to teach it. Ask them to conduct classes in the target language and to combine lecture with hands-on instruction. If the local Red Cross, clinic, or hospital isn't experienced in teaching such classes, use your copy of *Where There Is No Doctor* to guide the class. Ask your mentor to help find someone who can teach such topics in the target language.

3. Cultural Notes

Medical beliefs, practices, and remedies offer a rich mix for getting the flavor of cultural differences. If you are in a non-Western society, you may encounter a totally different way of viewing health care. Sometimes it may exist as a system by itself; sometimes it will be overlaid with Western health care ideas. Initially, exposure to some beliefs may be closed to you because Americans are perceived as nonbelievers. Some practices may have been the target of Western-oriented attempts to eradicate not only disease, but also traditional health care systems and even health beliefs themselves. To explore health care beliefs, start with the questions below.

What causes illness or disease? Are medical problems believed to be caused by germs or by other agents, such as improper acts or retribution by spiritual forces? (Disease or illness thought to be caused by other forces will probably have treatments that don't rely on medicine.) What are some of those treatments? Can one prepare oneself to cope with a theoretical illness such as a presupposed cut, scrape or bout with pneumonia? Can one plan for illness?

Who treats illness or disease? (While you may be used to consulting a physician, a druggist or medical practitioner, in many societies others are deemed qualified to treat what you perceive to be medical problems.) Are they specialized or general practitioners? What problems do they treat?

How does one treat illness or disease? (Your friends probably know of locally accepted cures or remedies unknown to you.) What do people recommend for common medical problems? How do those treatments work? How are people with special problems, such as mental illness, treated?

4. Spin-Off Activities

Local hazards. Learn to treat common problems caused by local hazards, such as the bite of a poisonous insect or animal, contact with poisonous plants, common wounds (such as coral scrapes or cactus punctures), and be aware of your reaction to certain foods or combinations of foods.

Add a section on local hazards and treatments to your first aid class. Begin with what you should stay away from. Include practical advice: don't swim in those waters because they are shark-infested! and the local equivalent of "leaves of three; let them be!" etc. Learn traditional antidotes and treatment for common hazards. For some problems, treatment using our system of medical care might not be available; for others, the local treatment might be more effective.

Local health problems. Explore health conditions in your new country. What are the major health problems? the leading causes of illness and death? How do those compare with the major problems in the U.S.? Look at problems of the very young (the incidence of children incapacitated by diarrhea, malnutrition, eye diseases) and problems affecting the elderly. Do specific illnesses or diseases exist which are rare in your own experience—malaria, schistosomiasis, kwashiorkor, encephalitis?

Likely sources of information on local health problems include the ministry of health or its equivalent, the state planning agency (with its development plans), and international development agencies, such as the World Health Organization, Agency for International Development, CARE, Red Cross.

Local medical care and remedies. In societies that have a strong tradition of non-Western health care, you can open your mind to different approaches to health care. As a local example, we have seen in the U.S. increasing interest in acupuncture, a medical technique that has existed for centuries in China.

Look into locally accepted treatment and products. Identify existing alternative health care systems. Are there specialists who treat certain problems, such as medicine men, faith healers, *curanderos* (folk practitioners with special knowledge of herbs and home remedies)? Do traditional remedies exist for illness, disease, and injury, for example, certain herbs and potions, special treatments, exercises, incantations? One doesn't have to convert to non-Western medicine to find local treatments that work well. On the other hand, even if you prefer to confine your own health care to Western medicine, you can still profit by the increased understanding that knowledge of local belief systems brings you.

5. Mini-bibliography

The Berlitz guides, *[...] for Travellers*, contain a useful section on doctors, which provides many medical and illness terms. Moran's drawings in *Lexicarry* (pp. 56-57) will help you and your mentor define body parts and some common medical problems. An excellent reference on personal health care is Werner's *Where There Is No Doctor*. For exploring the community's health conditions, see Darrow and Palmquist, *Trans-Cultural Study Guide* (pp. 130-42).

SAMPLE LESSON SIX
Did He Say It's to Eat, Sit on, or Play with?
or Figuring Out the Meaning of an Unfamiliar Word

Earlier lesson plans in this chapter focused on the language of practical situations. On occasion, however, you will find yourself up against a new concept, rather than a new physical setting. Sometimes you will want to express ideas for which you don't have the vocabulary. At other times you will hear words for concepts you don't understand. Preparing for these occasions is different from preparing for a predictable situation. This lesson plan demonstrates how to use the learning cycle to prepare for dealing with new concepts.

1. The Daily Learning Cycle

Decide. In most conversations, no matter what the context or setting, people use words unfamiliar to you. Sometimes the meaning is clear from the context; many times it is not. Some words you remember and can ask your mentor about later. Many, you forget. You need a way to define words on the spot. Let's learn how to do that.

Prepare. You have noticed that unfamiliar words seem to crop up in at least three recurring patterns: (1) unfamiliar things (nouns)—He was studying the [*betia*] when ..., (2) unfamiliar actions (verbs)—He stood on the corner with the old men, [*pagngumanganga*] like a native, and (3) unfamiliar qualities or attributes (adjectives)—Their [*agraciado*] movements fascinated me.

In each case, the term wasn't something you went looking for. Rather, the words popped up in normal conversation. Using one activity as an example, develop an exercise that will help understand the meaning of such words. Try something like the following:

> **Speaker:** *Let me tell you one! Here I am, just minding my own business, pagngumanganga, when ...*
> **Learner:** *Pardon me, Tobutu, did you say pagngumanganga? What does pagngumanganga mean?*
> *[Look of disbelief—after all, everyone knows what pagngumanganga is—followed by rapid, unintelligible explanation.]*
> **L:** *I don't understand. What were you doing? pagngumanganga? Is it ... something men do?*
> *[Sigh, shrugging of shoulders, and another explanation]*
> **L:** *Is pagngumanganga similar to [eating lunch]? When you pagngumanganga are you [sitting]? Do you*

pagngumanganga like this (pantomiming)? Do you
pagngumanganga [in the marketplace]? [with a group of
people]? Show me what people do when they
pagngumanganga!
[Demonstration. Laughter all around.]
> *L: OK, I think I've got it. Pagngumanganga means [chewing*
> *betel nut], right?*

Practice. Using the following activities, practice until you can
respond to an unknown term with rapid-fire questions:

- Questions for defining an activity. Develop and practice a drill
  with your mentor that helps you define an unknown activity by
  asking questions. Try to phrase your questions using the unknown word as often as possible. Repeating it frequently will help
  drive it home in your mind.

  Use questions such as, "Is [...] something that women do? Is
  [...] similar to [eating]? Do you [...] like this? Do you [...] at any
  particular time or place?

- Questions for defining things. Develop sample questions and
  possible approaches to defining things. For example, you might
  develop questions involving description (What does a [...] look
  like? Is there a [...] around here? Can you show me a [...]?),
  location (Are [...] found near a house? in the village?), comparison with other things (Are they physical items like meeting
  houses, churches, etc.?), or use (What does a [...] do? What is
  a [...] used for? Who uses a [...]?). Or you might ask someone to
  sketch one for you, take you to one, bring one to you, etc.

- Questions for defining attributes. Develop questions and possible approaches for defining attributes or characteristics. For
  example, Is [...] like [something you know]? What other things
  can be [...]? Can people be [...]? Animals? Am I [...]? Is [...] a
  good thing to be? Can you demonstrate [...]? Why is he considered to be [...]? Ask for a demonstration.

Wokabaot. These questions help you elicit a definition during an
ongoing conversation. Keep them in mind on your wokabaot. When a
new word pops up, break into the conversation with an appropriate
"Excuse me, did you say [...]?" and you are off and running.

You may also use your questions to create conversations. Keep
your eyes open for interesting activities, actions, or sights. When you see
something unusual, approach the individual or group with "Good morning! What are you doing?" or "Excuse me, what is that?" Ask as many
questions as you need to complete your understanding of the activity or
object. Repeat the word often to drive it home. Along the way, greet a

friend and describe the word you have learned. Use your new word and your questions with her to expand your understanding of the term.

Evaluate and Practice. Discuss the wokabaot with your mentor, modify your questions and add others as needed. Then do the following:

1. Commit the new terms to memory with short descriptions, definitions or role plays.

2. Have your mentor record the questions, definitions, and examples of the terms as used in conversation.

3. Agree on follow-up activities.

4. Decide on general objectives for the next session.

2. Supplemental Activities

Use the following exercises for additional practice.

Definition guessing game. Play a modified "twenty questions" with your mentor. Ask him to tell you a word that represents a thing, action, or attribute he thinks you don't know. Question him until you understand the word's meaning. Test your understanding further; use the word in new sentences and get your mentor's reaction.

Word identification game. Play charades to learn terms for actions or things you have seen but don't understand. Perform an action. Use gestures to draw an image of what you have seen or an attribute for which you want to know the correct word. Let your mentor give you the word, then a brief definition or explanation (in the target language).

3. Cultural Notes and Spin-Off Activities

Word definition goes beyond simple explanation of word meaning. A major benefit of living in another culture comes in participating in activities new to us (chewing betel nut or bathing in a public bath house, for example) or experiencing familiar events in totally different ways (celebrating a marriage). Seeking definitions extends beyond language to experiencing culturally different events in which both the language and the activity itself are new. Try the following:

An indigenous social event. The tools, protocol, manners, interaction patterns and language of a group of men chewing betel nut are different from a group of guys in the U.S. sitting around drinking beer in the back yard on the Fourth of July. As you participate, ask questions that help expand your understanding of the event. For example, "What is the white powder you are using?" "It's lime? Where do you get the lime?" "What is the leaf that you chew with the lime?" "How much of each do I use at one time?" "What does the tree look like that it comes from?" "What is the bag called that holds the lime?" etc.

How one drinks *kava* in Fiji, *toddy* in Kiribati or *tuba* in the Philippines differs in each society. Feasts and banquets in different societies consist of strikingly different foods, prepared differently. Join in such activities and learn to describe, explain, and interpret as well as participate appropriately.

An indigenous work event. Each field of employment develops a specialized vocabulary that is usually unfamiliar to the uninitiated. Just as a nonprinter may find little meaning in the distinction among *em*, *en*, and *pica*, so will Western landlubbers be unaware of the range of terms that describe parts of a Gilbertese canoe, changes in wind direction and velocity, or a canoe's reaction to different currents and wind conditions.

Participate in activities that haven't been part of your background: canoe fishing in the ocean; building a palm-leaf roof or the tied and woven house that fits beneath it; tending and harvesting rice, olives, or taro; preparing daily meals over an open fire. Join tours where *sake*, wine or beer are bottled, then join in discussion of how drink fits into daily life. Visit the modern factories which turn out the export products, meet some of the employees, and talk about the relationship of worker to employer and worker to product. Mingle with artisans—glass blowers, potters, cabinet-makers—and learn the tools, heritage, and psychic rewards of their trades.

Your set of questions will become invaluable for defining what is happening around you and why.

4. Mini-bibliography

See "Linguistic Fundamentals" in the references for chapter 6 for additional linguistic skills to consider. Larson's *Guidelines for Barefoot Language Learning* (pp. 139-59) suggests activities for classifying, defining, differentiating, mapping, and establishing sets of words.

Six

Techniques and Topics:
Where Do I Go When the Pavement Ends?

Cuernavaca, city of eternal spring, for decades refuge from the sweltering summer heat, gagging pollution, and chaotic busyness of Mexico City, is a city of language schools. Cuernavaca yearly draws thousands of young Americans who flock to a finely tuned industry that offers in two months Spanish-language skills unattainable in a year at most universities.

We watched the students one summer. Some were classmates; others we met between classes, at parties, on weekend excursions to Acapulco, Ciudad de Mexico, Taxco, Oaxaca.

Many of us gained in Cuernavaca, not honed skills in Spanish, but new friends—other American and Mexican students with whom we debated U.S. imperialism and Mexican poverty. On pleasant afternoons we expanded our new-found knowledge of Mexico's rich cultural, architectural, artistic, and political heritage.

We endured the small classes. We looked forward to hourly breaks and friendly chatter over *pan* and rich, black *cafe* at the small tables on the stone patio. In English, many planned weekend escapes. Prodded by insistent teachers, we trudged back into the classroom cubicles and struggled together to perfect our accented Spanish and expand our tiny vocabularies.

Many students shared apartments; others rented houses. Some

stayed with Mexican families, where often they found (much to their relief) that an elder son or daughter spoke English more fluently than they had ever hoped to speak Spanish.

We drilled, memorized, stuttered. Our heads swam. We discovered that language learning is hard work. Just being in Cuernavaca did not guarantee proficiency; Spanish didn't seep in as we slept. We all learned some Spanish; none of us mastered it. We enjoyed the sights and our experiences, but we scarcely tapped the wealth of learning opportunity that surrounded us.

Our Cuernavaca experience was not unique. How many hundreds of Americans have returned from working or teaching in Germany or Costa Rica or Kenya with a few greetings and a bit of cocktail chatter in German, Spanish or Swahili? We know committed and hard-working Peace Corps volunteers who, after two years, left villages and rural schools able to cope with only the simplest needs in the local language, and professionals who lived abroad with their families for several years and learned no more than a smattering of greetings and small talk. (Happily, we know others who have come away fluent.)

Living abroad can provide an environment which encourages language learning, but it does not **automatically** lead to immersion in the culture or to language fluency.

Strong forces work against our mastery of another language in a foreign setting: the sheer effort it takes; the many people worldwide who speak English; our own ethnocentrism; our need for the familiar and comfortable which draws us to other expatriates.

These needs are real. Don't ignore them. Just as language learning teaches the importance of culture, so does living abroad throw into relief your own cultural heritage. You will want to discuss ideas beyond your target-language ability, read an English-language magazine, write an American friend, enjoy an American meal, chat in English, and explore in depth your cross-cultural experience. Feel free to set aside language practice from time to time. Recognize that while you strive to learn a new language and understand a different society better, you remain a person of your own culture.

But don't let yourself be captured by the Cuernavaca syndrome. Your constant thrust should be toward speaking the target language and living cross-culturally. This chapter suggests ways to maintain that thrust by tapping the local environment for language learning.

The challenge facing a self-directed language learner is how to move beyond the prepared course—whether it be an immersion program, language class, text, private tutor, or introductory set of self-directed lessons—and continue learning on your own.

The lesson plans in chapter 5 illustrate the daily learning cycle.

They focus on key survival language. When you have mastered those six lessons, you will be on your way toward being able to use key grammatical structures in your daily conversation, identify your individual needs, and undertake appropriate follow-up activities.

Remember that you won't become fluent overnight. Language learning is a process; for most of us, it's a long one, a hard one. The constant drilling and repetition needed to learn even basic structures is tiring. Venturing daily into the community and confronting new situations can be exhausting.

The key is to break down what appears to be an overwhelming job into smaller tasks. Lay out realistic steps that move toward identifiable goals. Then, tackle each a week at a time. Ask yourself these two questions:

1. Do I approach my language study systematically?

You need to move gradually from simple language skills to more complex ones. Perhaps you can master a language in sporadic bursts of creative energy, waiting until the spirit moves you to study. But most of us can't; we need planned, organized, continuing, regular work toward identifiable goals. The password is *systematic*.

2. Have I set aside daily time to study language?

Fluency comes not as a bolt from heaven, but from accumulated hard work. Simply setting aside time is important.

Timing is also important. Does language come more easily for you early in the morning? in the afternoons or evenings? in short stretches of thirty minutes? in four-hour blocks? Determine the best part of day for you, and your optimum amount of study time. Then make sure you set that time aside just for language—and that you continue with it.

To help you plan your own lessons, this chapter provides three important aids:

1. **Interaction hints** for taking full advantage of the immersion opportunities that exist when you live abroad.

2. **Techniques** that add variety to your learning. They include a set of mini-lesson plans—simple, short, step-by-step activities that teach practical skills—and hints that help increase the productivity of your language activities.

3. **Topics** from which individual learning cycle lessons can be developed. Each topic is broad enough for several lesson plans, yet specific enough to suggest immediate learning activities. Think of each as the germ of a full-scale language module. For each you need to define performance objectives, develop a sample passage, practice the passage using appropriate drills and exercises, try the passage in a wok-

abaot, review the experience, revise your passage, and undertake follow-up activities.

One caveat: chapter 5 lesson plans are detailed enough for the beginning language learner. If you have the time and inclination to write comprehensive lesson plans, do so: detailed plans direct and add clarity to your learning. Be forewarned, however, it takes time to think through, write, revise, and polish good detailed lessons. Whether you prepare lengthy written exercises or whether you use the topics as ideas and prepare your lesson plans mentally, keep in mind that your goal is to learn the language, not write about it. Use whichever approach best helps you meet your language learning goals.

PART I: HINTS ON INCREASING INTERACTION OPPORTUNITIES

WREST MORE HOURS FROM A BUSY DAY

"But where will I find the time I'm supposed to be organizing?" you might ask. Good question.

If you work full time, you have to cram more activities into a day that may already be overwhelming.

If you are an unemployed spouse (that is, someone who receives no monetary remuneration for your work), you must establish a home, raise a family, and negotiate day-to-day life in an unfamiliar setting. Your challenge is to carve out time for language study from a full day devoted to family support.

Let's address the needs of the employed and the unemployed separately.

Expanding Time: Hints for the Employed

Begin work as a full-time language student. Many employment conditions are negotiable: salary and such benefits as travel, housing, training. Try to negotiate time to study language before you start work; two months spent on language acquisition, you can argue, will benefit not only you but your employer (and his customers, clients, beneficiaries). If work absolutely must begin on a certain day, negotiate to arrive in-country two months early (at your employer's expense, of course).

Naturally, your employer wanted you four months ago. Your work demands so much you will never catch up. You are dying to tackle the job, and you feel pressured to produce. Look at it objectively. Your employer has survived without you for years. What, really, is another two months?

Is two months impossible? Go for a month—still enough time to get your language learning off to a running start.

Negotiate daily release time. Are work demands too great to allow full-time study? Accept the job, but spend the first two hours each morning in language learning. Or knock off at 3:30 each afternoon for two uninterrupted study hours.

Get double duty from your work time. If you are a skilled laborer, practice language while you work (lay a brick, count to ten; lay a brick, describe aloud your actions, etc.). If your skills are less tangible (managers, teachers, etc.), squeeze your on-the-job language study into moments when communication is less important, for example, the walk to the restroom, pencil sharpener, or filing cabinet; those moments spent daydreaming or planning evening activities. Use those moments to speak silently, describe, question, drill yourself. They add up. Also try the following suggestions.

First, practice at work. As soon as you communicate well enough to perform your job, urge coworkers to speak to you only in their language. (Actually, you can begin sooner: you need not understand all of every conversation with every employee. Identify those with whom you have leeway, e.g., those in other departments, someone else's secretary, etc.; with them emphasize language practice over understanding.)

You can also practice on breaks. Arrange language practice with coworkers during coffee or tea time; set aside the lunch period for conversation as well as sustenance.

Third, practice while commuting. If you drive, talk to yourself. If you walk or take a bus, chat with others. Find a coworker who lives in your direction, travel together, and use the time for language practice. Or work by yourself in vocabulary building with small sets of cards.

At work or at home, those empty spaces can add hours of practice to your daily routine. Don't wait for planned language time to practice language.

Look for job-related language learning opportunities. Find work projects that can expand your language ability. If you are well along the road toward language mastery, perhaps you can write or translate a personnel or project manual into the target language, create a training program for host country staff, or translate government regulations from bureaucratese into colloquial prose.

Training others or preparing training materials can provide excellent language practice. Don't wait until you are fluent; team up with a native speaker. Your language ability will improve dramatically in the process.

Creating Time: Hints for the At-Home Spouse

In the past the unemployed American female living overseas who was neither student, indigent artist, nor heiress, was a wife. She accompanied her soldier, businessman, teacher, or government husband. She raised the kids, kept house, entertained, ran errands and somehow created a meaningful life as a support person. Often she had little choice in the matter, and frequently, neither cultural orientation nor language training.

Many women (and increasing numbers of men) still find themselves in this position. If you are among them, this section is for you.

Dropped into a strange society, you are left to your own wits. Daily treks to the market replace your weekly trip to Safeway. You may wash clothing by hand, or find, hire, and supervise household staff. Routine errands take hours. What with setting up a new household, scrounging up the furniture that was promised but never came, finding sources for your basic consumables, child care, and schooling, your desire to carve out time even to consider language study may seem unrealistic.

Your task differs strikingly from that of your employed spouse. You must create a structure which fosters learning. The trick is one of perspective: you need to fit language study into your daily routine rather than add time to an exhausting day. Difficult? Yes, but try the following.

Set aside language learning time. It is crucial that you reserve time to study language in the first days of your stay. This is when demands on your time are the greatest, when errands are all-consuming—and when you set the patterns that will become your routine during your stay abroad. Set aside language learning time first in order to rest from the treadmill of settling in. Set a tone that enforces your belief that language learning is important.

Organize your routine as grist for language study. Your daily routine presents opportunities to learn language; use it to your advantage. You have to shop, for instance, but don't just go shopping. Go on field trips to the market and use them as language learning experiences. Survey your impending tasks—meal preparation, child care, staff management, sightseeing—and organize language learning activities for each.

Capitalize on your role as a support person. Plan and supervise a language learning program for your spouse. Chances are he or she will feel inundated at work, unable to follow through on language study. By developing your spouse's program—thinking up topics, creating drills, organizing sessions, finding and working with mentors—you will hasten your own language learning. Helping your spouse sharpens your own language ability. You will become your family's best target language speaker.

JUMP INTO THE POOL BEFORE YOU CAN SWIM

In general, the more you interact with local folks in their language, the more quickly you will master the language. And the better you speak the language, the greater your opportunities will be to participate in a broader range of activities. You don't have to speak fluently, however, before you begin talking with people. You can develop friends and build language ability at the same time.

Use life's necessities as language practice. Unless you live in a five-star hotel with a rich expatriate aunt, or are chained up inside a barracks or student dormitory, life abroad means you will spend time shopping. You need bread, wine, and cheese; toilet paper, toothpaste, and soap; stamps, envelopes, and writing paper; maybe a new shirt, skirt, or sandals. Or you may want to find a friend's house, catch a bus to a nearby city, or tour a castle.

When you do venture out, don't run errands; go on language learning excursions. Buy bread at the *boulangerie*; cheese at the *fromagerie*; your soaps and toiletries at the *parfumerie*. Avoid the supermarket. It takes more time. It is more hassle. It also creates opportunities to talk to people, to practice, to gain fluency.

In short, don't spend Saturday morning shopping. Make Saturday's language class a field trip to the nearest commercial strip. Buy a few items as your language exercise.

Buy your stamps at the central post office, even if you can use the APO system. It takes longer, but the reward transcends language learning. Think of it as buying year-round Christmas presents. Your stateside friends will enjoy a letter adorned with an exotic foreign stamp much more than one mailed with the same boring stamp they got last week from Chicago.

Dine at restaurants frequented by local people rather than by tourists. Local cafes are cheaper as well as being good places to practice reading and speaking. If you are a bit daring, order at random. You will quickly learn the names of various dishes. If you cannot tolerate hunger pangs, carry a sandwich for those times you order something you just can't get down. (Wouldn't you think, for instance, that *beche-de-mer* would provide an exotic entree to a lovely evening? Alas, for the uninitiated, the sea slug serves better as a stimulant for conversation than it does delight for the taste buds!)

In summary, creatively meeting your survival needs provides language practice in its cultural context. Structure your chores into learning opportunities.

Engage in a social life that both fits your style and reinforces your language practice. Recreation and relaxation preferences differ. Some of us read; others climb mountains or scuba dive. Some of us thrive on competitive sports: tennis, football, hockey, cribbage. Others think joy comes on a bar stool, guzzling a brew and lamenting the ways of the world with our fellow swizzlers.

Whatever your preferences, recreation offers opportunity to meet people and expand your language ability in specialized areas. Try joining a local sports club, for example. If your sport isn't among the local fare, try something different: soccer, *Te Ano*, cricket, lacrosse, rugby, quoits. Even if you are chosen last in pickup games, you will at least meet people and learn new terms. If you play poorly (and your teammates take the game seriously), you can learn swear words (a vital part of your listening vocabulary).

Another idea is to volunteer your services for a worthy cause. Spend time with orphans, at a day-care center, youth club, adult education center, hospital, library, or historical society. Contribute, as you would at home, to the betterment of society, and make friends while you are at it.

If you have the inclination, you can visit local pubs. You will find establishments where *gringos* (or *haoles* or soldiers or *gaijin*) aren't welcome, so make the rounds carefully, preferably with a local guide.

If music is your interest, find a musical group, regular jam session, choir, or coffee house. If you sing, play a mean guitar, flute, or panpipe, you can make acquaintances by the score. Add local favorites to your repertoire, and your musical flair will win many friends.

If you are a churchgoer, your religion offers a passport to a family of believers with a myriad of activities and a body of specialized language as well as a congregation of people. If you are not a churchgoer, become one. Churches offer social, cultural and language experiences as well as religion.

Try learning a local board or card game. Whether it's checkers, chess, *warri*, or Parcheesi, watch first to learn the rules. Have a friend teach you the basics. You have added a pastime, vocabulary, and another window on the language.

One more suggestion is to take advantage of live arts, entertainment, and social events. The potential is enormous: theater, concerts, opera, special arts festivals, holiday feast days, weddings, coming-out and birthday parties, wakes, arts and crafts fairs, school presentations, recitals, lectures, folk festivals and folk-group concerts, saints days, etc.

Each of the above activities offers special language forms and different ways to meet people. Seek them out—beginning with those which fit your own lifestyle—and use them to expand your language-speaking ability.

Enroll in a traditional language class. Be broad-minded as well as eclectic. If you believe the structure and direction of a traditional, teacher-directed language class will help you, sign up. Attend faithfully. Work hard in class. Do your homework. The regular schedule will focus your study, expand your vocabulary, and, perhaps, sharpen your speaking and listening skills.

A note of warning: don't let formal classes replace learning. Don't enroll, congratulate yourself, and assume your language needs will be met. You must study diligently after class if you expect to master your target language. A traditional language class, at best, provides an appetizer to learning; it is not the whole meal.

Spend time with people of different age groups. Children and elderly people can be excellent resources for the language learner. Both have time to converse, and both can be enticed to speak slowly enough to be understood.

Children use basic grammatical structures and can teach simple songs and local games.

One beauty of old age is that old people recognize the value of unhurried conversation. Throughout the world, they gather to exchange pleasantries; they stroll about; they sit, rock, observe. Many have time for you.

PUT YOURSELF INTO THE LINE OF FIRE

One major advantage of living abroad is that your target language permeates the environment. The atmosphere itself is ripe for the plucking of language instruction.

Your first days abroad provide an ideal time to tune into a multitude of possibilities. Notice how reading opportunities leap out at you en route from the airport: billboards and marquees, street signs, shop window displays, newspaper stands, and bus advertisements provide a cornucopia of instruction.

Listen as sounds inundate you: blaring radios and television sets; hawkers, street vendors, public address systems; a babble of voices in buses, on the streets, in cafes. Ride the *Strassenbahn* or metro. Listen to that couple behind you, to the four businessmen at the next restaurant table, to the animated sparring of a vendor and customer in the fresh fish section of the market. Haunt locales where the *université* crowd hangs out. Focus your listening: a buzz of spoken chatter eventually becomes identifiable words and sentences. As your new surroundings become familiar, your mind will tend to shut out the babble of noise and the panoply of sights. Don't let it! Allow yourself to be open to the flow of language around you.

Tune in local radio news programs and talk shows. Leave the radio on as a backdrop that subconsciously attunes your ear to the flow of the language.

Record sample news programs and play them back. If you are a beginner, try to identify single words among what seems to be gibberish. If you are further along, try to catch the main idea of each news segment. If you are quite good, you can even practice speaking with the announcer.

Watch television. Look for international news and weather shows with their familiar visual props, style and content. Watch children's programs with their simpler vocabulary and sentences. Watch game shows and learn idiomatic speech. Find dubbed American reruns. Since you know the actors, plot, and dialogue, you can concentrate on the words.

Listen to popular music. Also memorize host country classics, folk, and children's songs.

Study billboards, street signs, store displays. Read labels. Pronounce the words aloud. (Then smile pleasantly at shoppers who stare at you curiously.)

Read newspaper headlines. Buy comic books. Find an educational bookstore or trade your favorite T-shirt to a neighborhood kid for school primers.

SETTLE INTO A LEARNING ENVIRONMENT

One of the quickest ways to immerse yourself in language is to move in with a non-English-speaking host country family. (Of course, if you are accompanied by your spouse and children, this may not be possible.)

A family setting nurtures language learning: chatting over breakfast and dinner, on the veranda for after-dinner coffee, on weekend excursions. You can practice with children, adults, and grandparents. You gain access to neighbors and friends, clubs and organizations, and get hints on where to shop, visit, sightsee.

Unfortunately, family living is not always easy. Irritation and frustration can mount from different living styles, personality conflicts, and cultural faux pas. Sometimes, too, family living may not encourage language practice. Some family members may insist on practicing their English rather than teaching you their language. And for beginning language students, sometimes the gap is too great.

Family stays can initially prove embarrassing when families treat foreigners as special guests. You feel guilty when no one lets you help with housework, meal preparation and cleanup; or when someone picks up after you; or when you get special service, sometimes special food. Generally, however, those problems diminish as your family and you work out the differing expectations for each other's behavior. Despite its difficulties—or perhaps because of them—family living offers language and cultural learning unavailable in any other way.

PART II: TECHNIQUES TO HELP YOUR LEARNING PROGRESS

The following section offers techniques that add variety to your language learning activities. First is a set of twelve techniques which can be used as lessons or as part of a lesson. Many of them suggest different structures and vocabulary. They can be used at a variety of learning levels, although some are obviously limited to specific levels of ability. Second are two sets of suggestions for increasing the effectiveness of your language learning, both within and beyond your formal language practice.

TECHNIQUES THAT ADD VARIETY TO YOUR LESSONS

Use Simple Drawings as Visual Aids

Drawings, photographs, and pictures can be effective learning aids. Even simple drawings such as penciled stick figures, a rising or setting sun, or a house can portray important ideas. They are easy to make. For example, learn basic greetings with this exercise:

1. On separate pieces of paper draw simple pictures representing the rising, setting, and midday sun; nighttime; and figures depicting male and female children, adults, and elderly persons.

2. Show the drawings to your mentor and verify that she understands each. Indicate that you want to learn the greetings for one period of the day for a particular type of person.

3. Have your mentor model the greeting. Practice it until you can say it fluently. Use appropriate pattern response drills and role plays to learn the greeting.

4. Using the drawings as cues, learn greetings for other periods of the day and other types of people. Follow the same procedures for each set of drawings.

This technique is particularly helpful to learn names of concrete objects. Equally effective are photographs from magazines, family photos, pictures in elementary and prereader workbooks and texts, picture books, and simple handbooks prepared by local agencies for use in villages. Or refer to your copy of Moran's *Lexicarry* and use his drawings on page 1 (see the references for this chapter). If you're into high tech, you can create your drawings with a Macintosh computer. And, if your extension cord is long enough, you will find the Macintosh a wonderful drawing card in a rural village.

Use Pictures for Perspective

Pictures and photographs provide tools for discussion. Often, they give new perspective to familiar scenes. Try this:

1. Choose a picture that represents a topic, a set of vocabulary, or a language structure you want to learn.

2. Show your mentor the picture. Ask him to describe in four or five sentences what he sees. Have him point out what he is describing as he speaks.

3. Have your mentor give the explanation several times. Then, repeat it. Practice sentence by sentence, using appropriate drills until you learn the entire passage.

4. Play with the description. Ask questions based on the passage you have memorized. Have your mentor ask you questions that you can answer using your memorized sentences.

If you are more advanced, try describing what is happening in the picture or make up a story about it.

Use Objects as Visual Aids

Objects are even better than drawings. This exercise identifies common small objects and presents simple sentences to refer to those objects.

1. Gather eight or ten familiar objects and show them to your mentor. Indicate that you want to ask "what is this?"

2. Listen carefully, repeat, and master the equivalent for "what is this?"

3. Using your target language, ask your mentor the name of each object. Repeat each term after your mentor identifies it. Practice each until you have learned them all.

4. Hide or cover one of the objects and indicate to your mentor that you want to ask "where is the [...]?" Have her pronounce the question for you. Listen carefully, repeat, and learn the question.

5. Hide or cover other objects and ask the same question, each time using the word for the hidden object. In some languages, different objects may require different types of questions; note carefully when your mentor indicates that the same question does not apply to a particular object.

6. Listen carefully for different forms of response, e.g., "Here it is!" or "The [...] is here." Repeat each answer until you feel comfortable with it.

7. Exchange roles and practice questions and answers until you become familiar with both.

8. Expand the exercise by moving the objects and eliciting responses used to indicate proximity, for example, "Here it is!" "There it is!" "There it is, way over there!"

9. Move the objects to create additional responses: "The [...] is next to the [...]." "The [...] is behind the [...]." "The [...] and the [...] are beside the [...]."

Unless you are Isis, Superman, or a magician, this exercise works best with small objects. As a variation, use large objects such as houses, people, trees, or the seashore by moving yourself rather than the object—"The [tree] is here." "Now, the [tree] is there!" This broadens your vocabulary and lets you stretch your legs while you learn.

At an intermediate level, you can describe a hidden object and see if your mentor can guess it, or vice versa. Or try playing "Twenty Questions."

Describe a Series of Actions

You can remember many common verbs more easily if you practice them as a logical sequence of steps. Try the following.

1. With your mentor, list no more than twelve actions you take each day in sequence, for example, "I wake up." "I go to the toilet." "I

wash my hands and face." "I …" Explain each action carefully (through pantomime if need be) to make sure both of you are clear on what the actions are. Have your mentor write down each item (in the target language).

2. Repeat the first three or four actions. Practice until you can repeat them easily without hesitation or mistakes. After you can recite the first group, continue through the list, adding one action at a time, and practice until you can repeat the entire list.

3. Review the actions—at the next session if necessary. Then, using photos or gestures, have your mentor give the sequence using a different pronoun, that is, if you began with "**I** get up," change it to **you** or **he**. If the changes do not cause significant changes in the verb, try to master the whole series at once. If the verbs change, practice three to four new sentences at a time until you can say all twelve.

To help keep the person you are referring to straight in your mind, use gestures to indicate *I, we, they* as you speak. Be careful to use culturally appropriate gestures; in some societies, pointing may be impolite or even hostile.

4. In later sessions, add modifiers such as *now, today, yesterday, tomorrow, last year*, which change the tense. Rely on the change in modifiers to signal your desire to change tenses; don't ask your mentor to identify the tenses involved or describe the structure of the new patterns for you. Such questions lead to **discussion about** the language, rather than **practice in** the language.

Use a "How To" Situation

Base a lesson on a technical task related to your work or everyday life. Because task-oriented situations require physical action, they provide excellent practice in verb usage. By using props as well as actions, you can quickly expand your vocabulary.

1. Choose a task you already know or are likely to perform; for example, tuning a motorcycle engine, cooking a local dish, planting a garden, operating a tape recorder. If you can provide props (an engine and mechanic's tools, the ingredients, a shovel, a tape recorder), your mentor can demonstrate the process or task as he explains it.

2. Ask a question that will initiate a demonstration, for example, "How do you fix it when it won't start?" or "How do you prepare the ground for planting?" Ask your mentor to show you how to perform the task as he explains.

3. Have your mentor demonstrate and explain the entire process

three or four times. Listen carefully so you can associate words with actions and objects.

4. Once you generally understand the explanation, stop your mentor after each two or three sentences. Attempt to repeat each set of sentences. Continue this way until you can explain and demonstrate the entire process.

5. In later sessions expand the usefulness of the topic by learning to explain the process as an event that occurred in the past or will occur in the future.

If the task is quite technical (such as repairing a motorcycle engine), break the overall job into a series of smaller tasks (changing a spark plug, checking for loose cable connections, for example). If you are not mechanical, you will quickly get in over your head in your target language if you try to explain a task that is too complicated.

Use Drawings of Simple Activities

The following drawing exercise teaches nouns and verbs related to a specific subject or technical skill.

1. Choose an activity that involves tools or implements, such as changing a tire on a car, digging a well, giving an injection.

2. Divide a blank page into six equal parts. Think of six objects related to the subject, for example, tire, wheel, hubcap, jack, lug wrench, nuts. Make a rough sketch of each object.

3. Identify each drawing for your mentor, and have her supply the appropriate word. Write the name of the object under each picture, including the proper article (*the, a, an*). Have your mentor repeat each word. Listen carefully and repeat.

4. Use each object in a sentence. Have your mentor correct your pronunciation and sentence structure.

5. Think up questions and answers for each drawing. Have your mentor correct you. Construct both positive and negative questions and answers.

6. Practice using the sentences. Ask the questions of your mentor, and have her ask the questions of you.

If you want to expand the exercise to improve your reading and writing skills, you can add the following.

7. Compose a paragraph-long story based on the structures, questions, and answers you have practiced. Create your story sentence by sentence orally, then on paper or a blackboard. Limit your text to six lines.

8. Read the text as you have written it. Have your mentor correct your pronunciation and syntax.

9. Slowly erase or block out words in each line (first nouns, then verbs, then adjectives, etc.) and reread the text after each series of erasures. Continue until you have erased the entire text and can recite the six lines from memory.

10. As review, have your mentor question you about the text.

Use Questions to Structure a Lesson

As you participate in or observe events that are new to you, you will develop questions about them. This is an excellent opportunity to learn the cultural significance of such events and the language that describes them.

1. Describe a situation for your mentor, using real characters known to both of you. For example, "Alioune's wife gave birth to a baby boy. They plan a special ceremony to celebrate the birth. Will you explain it to me?" Ask your mentor to explain the ceremony. Ask her to explain it again, several times if necessary, until you understand generally what happens at the ceremony.

2. Ask your mentor to list and describe the objects necessary for this ceremony. Listen carefully, and repeat the name of each object several times. Develop a mental image of each.

3. Ask your mentor what people (relatives, friends, officials) will be involved in the ceremony, either as participants or as guests.

4. Ask your mentor to explain how each object will be used and what each person's role will be. Again, listen carefully and ask your mentor to repeat each step and each role for you.

5. Ask your mentor to act out what different people will say to each other on this occasion. If you can, play each role.

6. Ask your mentor to describe what constitutes a successful ceremony. Listen carefully for descriptive words (e.g., well-attended, tasty, plentiful, fun-filled).

7. Try to summarize the ceremony for your mentor. Describe the process, the different roles taken, who will be present, and what makes it a successful ceremony.

8. Create, practice, and master a short passage that describes such a ceremony or poses questions about it that will enable you to obtain information from others and so better understand the ceremony.

This exercise is useful both before and after the ceremony. Use it before to focus your attention on key moments during the ceremony. Use it after you have attended a ceremony to better understand what you have seen and heard.

Deliver a Lecturette

A lecturette works best if you stick to a short time period and limit the vocabulary and structures presented. You will need a watch with a second hand and, preferably, a third person to serve as timer.

1. Ask your mentor to speak to you for exactly one minute on a topic that interests her. (Be considerate; give her time to compose her thoughts before she begins.)

2. Have her speak on the same topic a second time, again for exactly one minute, using the same structures and vocabulary as much as possible.

3. Ask her to repeat (patient woman that she is) a third time, again within the one-minute limit.

4. Ask your mentor about words or structures you didn't know.

5. Have your mentor ask you questions about what she said to see if you understand the passage.

6. Try to repeat, also within one minute, exactly what your mentor has said. Try to use the same vocabulary and sentence structures, asking your mentor to help you when you get stuck.

7. Record your mentor's talk on a cassette recorder and practice it later.

Tell a Popular Folktale

Folktales reflect the wisdom and rules of a culture. As your language skills improve, you will find folktales an entertaining source of language usage and cultural information.

1. Ask your mentor to tell you a popular folktale. As you listen, note particular gestures, facial expressions, changes in tone or volume, pauses, repetitions that make the telling of a folktale different from normal conversation.

2. Ask your mentor to tell the folktale several times until you understand the general story and its main lessons. Note particular phrasing that is different from normal discourse, and have your mentor explain key double entendres and references to historical events, tradition, cultural values.

3. Practice telling the folktale yourself. Develop drills to remember key phrases and punch lines.

4. Ask your mentor to record the folktale for you so that you can listen to it and practice it on your own. (It will also serve as a fond addition to your memorabilia collection.)

5. As a review the next day, tell the folktale to your mentor.

6. As follow-up, choose a folktale popular in the United States (an Aesop's fable, Paul Bunyan, Uncle Remus, Casey Jones, Peter Rabbit, for instance) and work out a shortened version in the target language. Encourage your mentor to correct your mistakes and ask questions both about your language and the meaning of the story. Record your presentation on tape. (It, too, will provide pleasant listening some winter evening years hence.)

Define Some Abstract Terms

Abstract terms such as *honesty, pride* and *courage* are difficult to define because frequently their definitions are based on different cultural concepts. Learning abstract terms brings not only increased language facility, but also insight into another culture. Try the following approach.

1. Ask your mentor to talk about persons who are admired in her society. When she seems to have found a fitting example, ask her what qualities this person is said to have.

2. Repeat this process several times, also eliciting descriptions of people who are not respected. Develop a list of terms describing common qualities and faults.

3. Study one term at a time. Have your mentor define the word (in the target language).

4. Once you have a general definition, determine its meaning more closely by proposing examples of situations in which you feel the word could logically be used. Have your mentor either approve or qualify your statement, for example, "Yes, [...] could be used in that situation." "No, one would have to do [...] or [...] for the term to be used in that context."

5. Ask your mentor for at least two examples of situations in which a person would be complimented for possessing this abstract quality. Ask for two examples in which a person would be criticized for not having this quality.

6. Ask your mentor to describe restrictions on the use of the word. Be alert for cases in which it might be considered offensive or insulting.

7. Develop role plays or drills that use the terms in their correct context and practice until you and your mentor feel comfortable with your use of them.

Translate a Simple Story

In general, we discourage direct translation from written English. It can easily lead to artificial structures and usage. As a variation, however, translations can give a needed break from the routine. Try the following.

1. Find a simple booklet or article on something of interest to you. Picture books or books written for beginning English speakers are especially useful because they contain simple language and colorful visual aids. Children's books work well too—if you don't mind the content.

2. Translate small units of three or four sentences orally into the target language, making sure you translate ideas rather than word for word. Have your mentor help you revise your translation into locally acceptable sentences with correct pronunciation.

3. Continue with small sets of sentences until you have completed the story or chapter that interests you.

Engage in Free Conversation

At times you and your mentor will just want to talk—no drills, no dialogues, no plan; just talk. Those times are precious. In general don't think of those times as part of your formal language session. Free conversation can be a valuable learning experience, but unless you encourage your mentor to correct your mistakes, free conversation will prove more interesting than useful as a language learning technique. To use free conversation effectively, follow these guidelines.

1. Choose a subject of interest to you and your mentor.

2. Ask your mentor to jot down errors rather than correct you during the discussion. (Constant correction breaks your train of thought and makes true conversation difficult.)

3. When you are finished talking, review the discussion with your mentor. Identify major errors, emphasize proper structures and vocabulary, and design appropriate follow-up drills to drive home the correct phrasing.

4. When your mentor points out an error, have him or her develop a new sentence using the correct structure, word or phrase. Repeat the new sentence several times. Then, transform the sentence into a

question and into a negative sentence. If your error was in vocabulary, use the word in another context. Try as many different sentences with the correction as you can.

SKILLS THAT WILL HELP YOU BE A MORE SUCCESSFUL LEARNER

In addition to the techniques presented above, you can develop skills that help make your learning more effective. Whenever you practice—at whatever your level of ability—keep the following in mind as you converse with others or practice on your own.

Master the Style of a Language Pro

As a learner you will have difficulty understanding people. They will have difficulty understanding you. The following hints can ease the transition from learner to conversationalist.

Show that you are paying attention to the conversation by giving steady feedback. Remember those "uh-huhs" that your parents bugged you about? Learn the target-language equivalents. They keep conversation going even if you can't phrase a response.

Ask people to repeat and/or speak slower. You won't always understand what people say; learn polite ways to ask them to repeat or to speak more slowly.

Speak simply. Use what you know. You don't have to speak elegant, poetic language to make a point. Use simple phrases and sentences, particularly if you are a beginner. Avoid sentence patterns or words which give you trouble. As you discover patterns that work, hang on to them. Use them again and again until you can blithely roll them off your tongue. Then vary them slightly and listen to your mastery grow.

If you are not understood, paraphrase. Your natural tendency is to repeat your words in a louder voice. Chances are, unless you were mumbling, speaking louder won't help. After repeating once, try a different approach.

Learn to gesture. The spoken word is part of a more complex communication system. Use your hands, eyes, and body to convey meaning. Watch how native speakers use their bodies; gestures are an essential part of communication and vary from culture to culture.

Learn the language fillers that native speakers use. Speakers of Waray-Waray (a Filipino language), for instance, have a handy word, *kwan*, to convey meaning when they can't think of the proper word, or when an imprecise word is satisfactory, for instance, "We were at the (kwan) when he came running up, eyes afire, tears streaming down his face." Fillers are used for words we can't think of, or to fill in time until we can think of the correct response or statement. In English we use such words as *thing, thingamajig, whatsit,* and *whatsername* when we cannot think of specific terms or names.

Use Mnemonics to Associate Words

Mnemonics are techniques to remember things by calling on familiar words to remind you of new words and their meanings.

Rhymes. Rhyming words (in the target language or English) help you recall other words. Memorize a new word, then think of one or two rhyming words that remind you of it; when you remember one, you will recall the others.

Alliterations. Words that begin with the same sounds can be remembered together, for example, in English, "from *stem* to *stern.*" Be sure, however, to associate each similar-sounding word with its proper meaning.

Onomatopoeia. Words that remind you of a particular sound help you form a mental image of their meaning, such as *buzz, hiss, cuckoo, boom.*

Cognates. Words in different languages that stem from the same root word help you build on your English vocabulary. Examples include *madre* in Spanish and *mother; kalt* (in German) and cold; *vacances* (in French) and *vacation.* Some words are borrowed from other languages, e.g., *boondocks* from the Tagalog *bundok.* They will expand your vocabulary.

Word and image associations. Words which fall into groups can be remembered by recalling other words in the same group or by associating them with mental images of what they mean. For instance, we can associate

- opposites: words thought of in pairs—hot-cold, wet-dry, etc.;
- synonyms: words with the same or nearly the same meaning—glad, joyful, happy;
- physical properties: words which indicate color, size, smell, feel, taste, etc.;
- function: words which indicate use—things for writing with, riding in, sitting on, etc.

Classes of words. Word classes are commonly taught in traditional language instruction—the numbers one through ten, days of the week, months and seasons of the year, holidays, colors, directions, family members, etc. As you learn one word, learn others from the same class.

PART III: TOPICS FOR LESSON PLAN DEVELOPMENT

As you analyze your language needs to plan follow-up learning cycles, you will find yourself approaching the task from different perspectives. No lesson plans exist to guide you. Your learning will now follow your moods and activities and the events in which you are involved.

The following learning topics flow from different ways of looking at language use. They are not progressive—you don't first master one set, then move on to the next! They are simply **different**. Use them as a bank of ideas to draw upon as your needs and progress dictate. Your language learning will encompass ideas from all five sets of language use below.

1. **Everyday situations**: language use based on real-life situations in which you find yourself. This is the approach we used to develop the first five lessons in chapter 5.

2. **Language structures**: language use that flows from the need to express yourself in normal conversation. Suggestions here are based on distinctly different types of sentence structures.

3. **Categories and word clusters**: language use based on the need to talk about objects, actions, events, abstractions, relationships, attributes. These suggestions flow from possible subjects you will want to talk about. This is the approach we used to develop the sixth lesson plan in chapter 5.

4. **Language nuance and clarity**: language use based on the need to express ideas clearly and precisely, including different shades of meaning as well as precision of expression. These skills include classifying, differentiating, and expanding words and sentences, as well as speaking fluidly, pronouncing correctly, and reading and writing at a survival level.

5. **Cultural appropriateness**: language use tied to the customs, values, and beliefs of the people with whom you are living. These suggestions tap the differences in language that flow from your being in a different culture.

Pick and choose from these categories. They provide a wealth of suggestions for daily learning cycle topics.

EVERYDAY SITUATIONS

One approach to choosing topics for a daily learning cycle is to anticipate likely situations you will encounter, then prepare yourself to deal with them. The following are examples of situations (other than those presented in chapter 5) that lend themselves to this approach.

Informal socializing: relating to host country people in informal situations—visiting; chatting together; carrying on "small talk"; drinking or partying; talking about common topics such as weather, current events, health.

Formal socializing: attending formal events such as banquets, feasts, receptions, cocktail and dinner parties, ceremonies; rites of passage such as baptisms, marriages, funerals.

Interacting with "family": relating to other "family" members in such day-to-day routines as mealtime behavior and conversation, household chores, sharing of household facilities, evening discussions, weekend activities.

Working: relating to coworkers on and off the job, performing your job, working with others on specific tasks, asking for advice or information, giving advice or directions, planning together.

Interacting with sales and service people: requesting specific items or services; asking questions about size, function, materials, costs; exchanging or complaining about goods.

Performing one's toilet: asking for facilities and performing basic personal functions in a culturally appropriate manner, including bathing, hair and teeth care, dressing and undressing, excretion.

Attending public events: attending such public events as sporting matches, concerts, political rallies, speeches, movies, dances, holiday celebrations, church services and special events; interacting with others in attendance; talking about the events in progress (or just concluded); buying tickets; performing appropriate rituals, such as singing the national anthem, praying, or cheering for the home team.

Using public transportation: getting around the city or country by airplane, bus, train, taxi, subway; making reservations and buying tickets; going through customs and immigration; hailing a taxi or bus; paying, giving directions to your destination; answering questions; identifying the appropriate bus line and bus stop; finding out departure or arrival times.

Communicating with public officials: carrying out business with public officials; asking for help from or answering questions of a policeman (for example, having witnessed an accident or crime);

discussing visa, health card, passport, or work permits with government officials; requesting and paying for public services such as government-owned housing, utilities, water and sewer, telephone.

Using public communications: using communications technology effectively; arranging for international telephone calls or telex; using the phone to carry out routine business; buying stamps and special services at the post office; receiving or sending international parcels.

Greeting and departing: appropriately meeting and leaving people; greeting friends and acquaintances at various times of the day; opening and closing conversations properly; saying goodbye and taking leave; introducing and being introduced to strangers, officials, friends of friends.

Dating and courting: relating appropriately to the opposite sex; carrying on "small talk"; asking for a date; paying compliments; entertaining; flirting properly; introducing friends, family, coworkers; participating in group events.

Performing: responding appropriately when called upon to publicly display some talent (or lack thereof). If you can, learn locally favorite songs in the target language. Other crowd-pleasers include reciting favorite traditional stories, legends, myths, fables, humorous incidents and jokes (at first using yourself as the butt of the joke). Learn also to play locally popular table, card, and word games.

Personal information: relating basic information on your personal history, family, education, interests, past jobs; describing and telling about yourself; asking others about themselves. Before those weighty discussions about world affairs, Western imperialism, the Communist threat, and man's relation to God, society, and his fellow man, it is useful to prepare conversations you will have as you get acquainted with people. Besides topics listed above, learn to describe your mother and father, your snow-covered house in Minnesota, and the '56 Chevy pictured in your snapshots.

LANGUAGE STRUCTURES

The above section organized possible language lessons in terms of potential situations. Another way to organize your learning is to examine different language structures needed to communicate in these situations.

Even if you weren't a whiz in high school English, you bring to your new language a broad understanding of English grammar. You have a sense of how at least one language works. Use that knowledge to expand your ability in the target language.

Questions: If you have ever flirted with becoming a journalist, you will recognize the "five Ws" in a flash—who, what, when, where, and why. They will give you information that expands both vocabulary and understanding. Can you ask such key questions as, "What is he doing?" "What is this thing?" "What is this used for?" "What did he say?" "Where are you going?" "Where did you go yesterday?" "Where is the market?" "Where do you buy eggs?" "When does the bus come?" "When are you leaving?" "Who is he?" "Who(m) did you invite?" "Why do we make the fire this way?" These are the basic types of questions; variations are endless.

Requests: Can you appropriately ask favors or request that certain actions be taken? "Will you help me?" "May I help ...?" "May I come with you?" "Would you give this to him?"

Orders: Can you give orders correctly? "Give that back!" "Take this to her!" "Finish the work in the kitchen, then ..."

Statements (positive and negative): Can you convey information, from simple to more complex? "This is a house." "I am an American." "The blue Austin-Healey beyond that ancient stable near Enrique's house belongs to one of his best friends." "I haven't studied German for five years." "They aren't usually home until 6:00 p.m." "I never eat after dinner." "The problem wasn't as bad as I thought." "I don't speak French."

Positive/negative responses: Can you make appropriate responses to questions, both affirmations and denials? "They *did* go with me." "No, they didn't go with me." "Yes, I would, thank you." "No, thanks, I'd rather not!" "No, he didn't!" "Well, yes, I think they will!" "No, I have no bananas."

Agreement: Do the different parts of your sentences fit together correctly? Do your subjects and verbs, nouns and adjectives, verbs and adverbs agree?

Voice: Can you use passive and active voice? "He was hit by the falling tree." "The tree hit him as it fell."

Polite phrases: Can you be appropriately gracious and polite? "Please!" "Thank you!" "No, thank you!" "Yes, I would, thanks!"

Time: Can you discuss and understand events occurring in different time periods? "I went yesterday." "I have gone three days this week." "I'm going now." "I plan to go tomorrow." "I had already gone when he called." And conditional variations such as, "I will go if he goes with me," "I would have gone if I had felt better," or "I would go if I weren't ill."

Ownership: Can you express ownership correctly? "Whose pen is this?" "That's my umbrella." "This is Julia's house." The biggest cookie is yours."

Description: Can you offer enough information for a listener to identify an object, an event, a person? "I'd like the green and white ball." "It was a huge tree with long, pointed needles. The bark was rough. The limbs drooped downward." "Who is that tall man with glasses?" "She was short, rather dumpy, with sparkling green eyes, thick, shimmering red hair that fell in great swirls to her waist, a button nose that ..."

CATEGORIES AND WORD CLUSTERS

A third approach to organizing your language learning is in terms of groups of words that describe objects, actions, events, abstractions, relations, and attributes. All vocabulary can be defined in some word cluster or concept category. Rather than attempt to classify everything you might possibly want to say, let us offer examples to stimulate your thinking.

Concrete objects: words that label things around you—those for people (men, women, children, boys, girls); buildings, houses, and their components (windows, doors, rooms); body parts (the common terms—head, eyes, nose, and legs, but also less frequently referred to but important words such as genitalia); places; foods; types of transportation; bodies of water; animals; clothing; etc.

Action words: words that describe things you will do or see others do—walk, run, swim, dig, build, sleep, eat, wash, sit, teach, work, play, rest—and the words for the key verbs that complete our basic sentences but don't express action—be, have, believe, seem, plan, intend, hope, etc.

Attributes: words that describe size, shape, color, position, location, feel, taste, sound, looks.

Possession: words that denote ownership (equivalents to his, mine, theirs), and words which indicate possession such as "the dog's tail," "the man's leg," "my book."

Prepositions: on, in, under, over, through, next to, etc.

Family and kinship: words that denote family relations—father, mother, son, daughter, grandparents, in-laws, godchild, niece; words for expressing role differences because of sex, age, status—elder, chieftain, matriarch, etc.

Pronouns: words used in place of people's names—he, him, she, her, they, them, it, I, me, anyone, everyone, this, that.

and young, authorities and citizens; appropriate ways to eat, dress, conduct oneself in public; topics you shouldn't discuss, questions you shouldn't ask, or places you shouldn't go?

Situational differences: Are you able to modify your language to fit different social situations? For example, do you know appropriate language for informal situations versus formal events; social class or position differences that require different language use, words of supplication or respect; professional gatherings and discussions that require specialized vocabulary and concepts?

Culturally related humor: As your language grows, you will be able to join in language-based humor. Can you understand (and then deliver) common jokes, puns, and wordplay; humor based on regional dialects, foreign accents and stereotypes; humor based on political and comic strip figures?

Allusions: Can you pick out and respond to indirect references to historical and current events, literary references? Can you understand and use idioms, proverbs, folktales?

SEASON THESE HINTS WITH A DASH OF PRACTICALITY

Immersion in another culture and language is no simple task. One doesn't suddenly cast off one's cultural self, forswear use of the native tongue, and cloak oneself in a new language.

As a practical matter, your language learning need not consume every minute of every waking hour. You don't fail if you speak English from time to time. In fact, your language learning should include breaks—both from slavish devotion to a single routine and from language learning in general. Do take time to discuss **in English** your cultural experiences with your English-speaking friends. Use your English to explore the meaning of living abroad, your frustrations and joys, your realization of those values and beliefs which make you American.

Our approach here should merely guide your language learning. Some suggestions may suit your learning style less than others. No problem! We advocate no single lock-step program. This approach will work if you follow its general thrust.

In summary, the language-learning potential of living abroad can best be realized if you

1. assiduously seek to interact with host country people **in their language**;

2. take positive, active steps to expand your language ability; and

Emotions and feelings: words that denote love, hate, fear, anger, sorrow, sadness, happiness, pain, disgust, frustration.

Direction and position: words that denote left, right; up, down; behind, ahead; east, west; top, bottom; inside, outside; back, front.

Frequency: always, never, sometimes, rarely, often, etc.

Measurement: mathematical words such as those for basic numbers, currency, adding and subtracting; words that describe distance (including such approximations as near, far, over there, close), size (big, little, huge, tiny, "four centimeters long"), weight, volume, parts and whole (half, all, some, the rest, a piece).

Time: words for describing length of time—day, week, month, year; for telling time—hours, minutes, seconds; for measuring time—a long time, short time, a few moments; for describing time—yesterday, tomorrow, next week, week before last, now.

Seasons: winter and summer; the names used for parts of the year based on local weather conditions—hot, dry, rainy seasons, "time of the monsoons," etc.

Vulgarities and slang: even if you don't use foul language yourself, you need a listening comprehension of that which is said to you. Obvious words are those for genitalia (proper words for vagina and penis as well as common expressions such as cunt and dick); excreta; sexual intercourse; prostitute; homosexual; general epithets (for example, son of a bitch, asshole). It's also useful to know the words in various contexts, such as insult, threat, or play: "You dirty [...]" or "You should have seen that [...]." Keep in mind that the severity of vulgarities differs from language to language; that is, while you may want a general translation of a term such as "you fucker," be attuned to vulgarities that when translated into English would be mild or meaningless in comparison to their insult in their untranslated state, for example, "Go to shit!" "You goat!" "Your mother's religion!

LANGUAGE NUANCE AND CLARITY

In addition to structures and word categories, effective communication includes the ability to manipulate the language in certain ways. As your skills increase, you will want to express shades of meaning, making your language more precise. You will also want to concern yourself not only with **what** you say, but **how** you say it. Consider the following.

Classification: Can you sort objects, events, attributes into related groups? "This is a fruit ... those are vegetables." "The Tinikling is a dance;

other popular dances are […] and […]." "[…] (acting in a certain way) means you are angry."

Differentiation: Can you distinguish among similar words which have different connotations? As an example of a concrete object in English, we know the difference among dress-, polo-, and T-shirts. In our target language, we initially learn "shirt." Can you distinguish among different types in your target language? The notion is the same for attributes. For example, in English we can describe someone as fat, chubby, large, huge, overweight, plump, chunky; each gives a different but related image. Learn to make such distinctions in the target language.

Expansion: Can you move from a simple to a more complex sentence? Can you add descriptive words to make the meaning more precise (for example, "a deep purple," "shimmering brightly in the sunlight")? clauses and phrases that add detail and precision (for example, The dead *okapi* was lying "behind the small hut," "in full view of the game warden.")?

Fluidity: Can you speak smoothly, without pausing to grope for words, with sentences constructed in a natural order? Can you get across your ideas without resorting to circumlocutions and devise an answer without basing it on the words used in the question? Is your vocabulary adequate to discuss the topics you wish to discuss?

Pronunciation: Can you speak correctly so that native speakers understand you clearly? Are there sounds you have difficulty pronouncing? Is your intonation correct? Do you use proper inflections? Do you stress words, sounds, and sentences appropriately?

Cultural comparison: As you become more fluent, language moves well beyond basic communicative ability. Can you counsel, persuade, negotiate, interpret, represent a point of view in an argument, describe and compare your culture and that of your target language? In such comparisons, can you discuss geography, history, the institutions, customs and behavior patterns, current events, and national policies and politics of the target language country?

Reading: While *The Whole World Guide* concentrates on speaking and listening skills, survival reading and writing are also important. Consider the following:

- Reading labels and tags: names, addresses, dates, building names, public signs such as "no smoking," "exit").

- Writing basic information: your name, address and telephone number.

- Recognizing the letters of the alphabet or symbols used frequently in a syllabary or character language.

- Reading commonly encountered messages or phrases: menu items, schedules, timetables, maps, signs indicating hours of operation, traffic regulations.

- Reading simple printed material: posters and flyers, simple instructions or directions, newspaper headlines and story titles.

- Writing simple instructions or answers: an invitation, directions to your house, answers on government forms or applications.

- Reading simple paragraphs: letters, invitations, short newspaper or magazine articles, newspaper advertisements.

CULTURAL APPROPRIATENESS

As one learns a language, particularly when immersed in a cultural setting, one learns not only words, sentences, and language structures, but also the customs, values, and beliefs of a people. How people do things, what is more important or less important, and how people relate to each other are reflected in language as well as in actions.

A fifth approach to assessing your language needs and setting your language goals is that of cultural appropriateness. How well does your language use reflect the cultural milieu of the country? We have addressed **survival language** (Can you conduct yourself appropriately in meeting your basic needs: can you ask directions, buy food, tip, use transportation and the telephone, purchase and bargain, do routine banking, etc.?) and **routine relations** (Can you act appropriately in common relations with others: make polite requests, accept and refuse invitations, offer and receive gifts, offer appropriate greetings and leave-takings, make introductions, apologize, express your wants and needs, etc.?).

Equally important to your language learning are the concepts, behavior, and language that are rooted in a society's culture. Consider the following as key components of your language learning program.

Nonverbal cues: Can you respond to (and send) appropriate nonverbal messages that accompany the spoken language? For example, do you understand and correctly use gestures, facial reactions, body stance or movement, distance and closeness, hesitation or avoidance?

Common taboos: Do you recognize common rules of etiquette, taboos, and sensitive topics and situations? For example, are you sensitive to proper public interaction between men and women, elderly

3. use a host of tools, ideas, and events to practice, practice, practice your target language.

At best, these suggestions should spark practical ideas which mesh with your own personality, your learning needs and learning style, and your time lines.

Preparation:
Getting a Head Start at Home

Too often, too little time exists to prepare for going overseas. Despite our best plans, word comes at the last minute— "Yes, the job is yours; we need you within the month!" Then follows a helter-skelter dash to complete a thousand tasks. We scribble lists. We work furiously. Even on the final night before departure we find ourselves occupied far into the night. Then, when the plane is in the air, only then, can we relax.

That period between notification and departure is hectic. But it is also exciting. We look forward with anticipation. We study and restudy the atlas, pour through what information we can find about our destination, seek from those who have been there any hint on "what it's like there."

Yet, in anticipation of life abroad, it is easy to overlook a simple, but important fact: besides gaining access to new adventures, you are leaving behind the comfortable and familiar. Preparation for departure means not only packing physical belongings, but tying up emotional loose ends. This process—leave taking—is a key prerequisite to being able to free your energy for the tasks ahead. No matter how pure your intentions, you cannot effectively learn if you are worried about people, things, or ongoing problems you have left behind.

This admonition, easily stated, is difficult to follow. Departure often requires making sure that elderly parents (or adult children) are secure;

that the house, though not yet rented or sold, is in the hands of a competent agent; that the family pets and plants have new homes; that client relationships have been brought to a successful conclusion; that legal affairs have been attended to—a proper will executed, a potential lawsuit resolved; that work projects have been completed or passed on to others.

Leave taking also involves an endless list of details, such as medical exams, inoculations and consultation; travel plans, including tickets, passports and visas, work permits, packing and shipping; anticipation and plans for life abroad, including shopping for clothing and other necessary items. It means making arrangements for possessions— house, car, belongings which may need to be stored or sold; notifying correspondents of your impending address change; ending or changing subscriptions; closing accounts and services; arranging for bills that will come after you leave. And the list goes on, seemingly forever.

For most of us departure means having said appropriate goodbyes to friends and loved ones, having taken time to visit again or drop a note to an ailing relative, having made a last trip to a favorite haunt.

Proper leave taking requires effort, consumes time. When have your efforts been enough? No easy answer exists. We can offer only the recommendation that leave taking become an integral part of predeparture activities.

Finding time to add language learning to your hectic predeparture days is not easily accomplished; yet, despite the myriad tasks to be taken care of and the stress of your schedule, language learning should remain a high priority. It has an immediately practical use: if you can speak a few key phrases the moment you step off that plane, life will be much easier. Beyond that, your ability to work language learning into your predeparture establishes a pattern that enables you to resume your study immediately upon arrival (a period no less hectic than predeparture). By beginning language study immediately upon arrival, you greatly increase the likelihood that you will continue with it.

This final chapter looks at language learning in the context of predeparture preparation and suggests ways to begin your language learning at home, amid the welter of activities.

ENROLL IN A LANGUAGE CLASS

If possible, enroll in a formal language class before you leave the U.S., preferably a full-time immersion program.

Formal classes force you to program definite language learning hours into your schedule. If you are a beginner, and have only a few weeks, formal classes will introduce you to the sounds and structure of the language, teach you a few basic words and sentences, and foster the notion that language learning will be an important part of your daily life in the months to come. If you are more experienced, classes will help polish your skills, and propel you into your new environment

LIVE "ABROAD" AT HOME

In the long run, immersion in a target language-speaking environment is necessary to foster fluency, control of idioms, and the natural rhythm characteristic of those fluent in a second language. But make the most of your resources here at home. In addition to formal language class (or even if you don't have opportunity for formal study because your target language is an uncommon one), begin in situ training by utilizing the rich resource of people from different ethnic backgrounds right here in the United States.

When we think of native speakers of foreign languages in the U.S., we think immediately of Spanish-speaking communities of the West, Southwest, Midwest, Florida, and New York. Cities such as Los Angeles, Miami, San Antonio, Chicago, and New York boast thousands of Spanish-speaking residents. In addition, throughout the nation in small towns in Wisconsin, Michigan, Colorado, and Idaho (most states in fact), we find clusters of Spanish speakers. Many have lived in their communities for generations; others have recently immigrated.

Our nation's linguistic richness by no means ends with Spanish, however. Our largest cities offer enormous language variety—New York, Boston, and Chicago in particular offer a multiethnic richness. Northern Wisconsin has its Germanic and Scandinavian communities, Maine its French population; thousands of Japanese- and Chinese-Americans live in such cities as San Francisco and New York.

Beyond the more widely known concentrations of ethnic communities, however, are a mosaic of peoples in most major American cities. Take Denver, for example, a city not renowned for ethnic diversity. In addition to a sizable Hispanic population, its residents include numerous Vietnamese, Laotian, Cambodian, and H'Mong immigrants, as well as Japanese, Chinese, Korean, German, Italian, French, Palestinian, Ukrainian, Filipino, Greek, and other communities. While many Americans no longer speak the languages of their forefathers, many tens of thousands do. Our melting pot, we find, is more akin to a tossed salad with rich nuggets of clearly identifiable ethnic and language strains than it is to a blended stew.

In any community with native speakers of your target language— and the U.S has many such communities—you have the potential to enlist native speakers as mentors and to conduct wokabaots into language-specific ethnic neighborhoods.

We make two assumptions here: (1) that in such neighborhoods men and women do exist who, if approached properly, will be willing to help local "foreigners" improve their language skills, and (2) that acceptance in such neighborhoods requires a much different attitude and demeanor than normally characterizes majority/minority relations in this country.

You must become learner and respectful outsider. Don't storm into another person's neighborhood asking questions or making demands. Instead, approach neighbors through a gradually expanding network of friends and confidants, just as you would if you were overseas. In the process, you will demonstrate an interest in, an appreciation for, and an acceptance of ways and experiences different from your own. And, you develop friends in abundance.

You may find people who resent such intrusion, just as overseas you may find people who have no love for Americans. But they are the minority of the minority. Them, you leave alone.

The point is, opportunities exist to learn from native speakers. You need not wait until you step off the plane to begin practical, interactive language learning. The in situ approach provides a structure, rationale, and exercises that enable you to begin your language learning in your own backyard.

How do you find mentors in the U.S.? Just as you would overseas: seek them out in their own communities. If you are in formal language classes and if you like the instructor, propose that she work with you as mentor outside the classroom. Or, ask her to help you identify other likely mentors in the community. If such classes don't exist (and you find commercial language programs such as Berlitz too expensive), go into the neighborhoods, meet people, and recruit them. If you don't know the location of a particular ethnic or language group in your neighborhood, use the Yellow Pages, the newspapers, and city hall to find out. Try the following:

1. Identify ethnic churches, associations, stores, restaurants as initial contacts to learn the general location of ethnic communities and/ or to identify people who can introduce you to target language-speaking populations.

2. Read back issues of local newspapers to learn of ethnic groups and ethnic events that might lead you to members of the appropriate target language groups.

3. Identify cultural appreciation, interchange, or study groups likely to have an interest in and knowledge of the appropriate target language groups. These include associations of returned Peace Corps

Emotions and feelings: words that denote love, hate, fear, anger, sorrow, sadness, happiness, pain, disgust, frustration.

Direction and position: words that denote left, right; up, down; behind, ahead; east, west; top, bottom; inside, outside; back, front.

Frequency: always, never, sometimes, rarely, often, etc.

Measurement: mathematical words such as those for basic numbers, currency, adding and subtracting; words that describe distance (including such approximations as near, far, over there, close), size (big, little, huge, tiny, "four centimeters long"), weight, volume, parts and whole (half, all, some, the rest, a piece).

Time: words for describing length of time—day, week, month, year; for telling time—hours, minutes, seconds; for measuring time—a long time, short time, a few moments; for describing time—yesterday, tomorrow, next week, week before last, now.

Seasons: winter and summer; the names used for parts of the year based on local weather conditions—hot, dry, rainy seasons, "time of the monsoons," etc.

Vulgarities and slang: even if you don't use foul language yourself, you need a listening comprehension of that which is said to you. Obvious words are those for genitalia (proper words for vagina and penis as well as common expressions such as cunt and dick); excreta; sexual intercourse; prostitute; homosexual; general epithets (for example, son of a bitch, asshole). It's also useful to know the words in various contexts, such as insult, threat, or play: "You dirty [...]" or "You should have seen that [...]." Keep in mind that the severity of vulgarities differs from language to language; that is, while you may want a general translation of a term such as "you fucker," be attuned to vulgarities that when translated into English would be mild or meaningless in comparison to their insult in their untranslated state, for example, "Go to shit!" "You goat!" "Your mother's religion!

LANGUAGE NUANCE AND CLARITY

In addition to structures and word categories, effective communication includes the ability to manipulate the language in certain ways. As your skills increase, you will want to express shades of meaning, making your language more precise. You will also want to concern yourself not only with **what** you say, but **how** you say it. Consider the following.

Classification: Can you sort objects, events, attributes into related groups? "This is a fruit ... those are vegetables." "The Tinikling is a dance;

other popular dances are [...] and [...]." "[...] (acting in a certain way) means you are angry."

Differentiation: Can you distinguish among similar words which have different connotations? As an example of a concrete object in English, we know the difference among dress-, polo-, and T-shirts. In our target language, we initially learn "shirt." Can you distinguish among different types in your target language? The notion is the same for attributes. For example, in English we can describe someone as fat, chubby, large, huge, overweight, plump, chunky; each gives a different but related image. Learn to make such distinctions in the target language.

Expansion: Can you move from a simple to a more complex sentence? Can you add descriptive words to make the meaning more precise (for example, "a deep purple," "shimmering brightly in the sunlight")? clauses and phrases that add detail and precision (for example, The dead *okapi* was lying "behind the small hut," "in full view of the game warden.")?

Fluidity: Can you speak smoothly, without pausing to grope for words, with sentences constructed in a natural order? Can you get across your ideas without resorting to circumlocutions and devise an answer without basing it on the words used in the question? Is your vocabulary adequate to discuss the topics you wish to discuss?

Pronunciation: Can you speak correctly so that native speakers understand you clearly? Are there sounds you have difficulty pronouncing? Is your intonation correct? Do you use proper inflections? Do you stress words, sounds, and sentences appropriately?

Cultural comparison: As you become more fluent, language moves well beyond basic communicative ability. Can you counsel, persuade, negotiate, interpret, represent a point of view in an argument, describe and compare your culture and that of your target language? In such comparisons, can you discuss geography, history, the institutions, customs and behavior patterns, current events, and national policies and politics of the target language country?

Reading: While *The Whole World Guide* concentrates on speaking and listening skills, survival reading and writing are also important. Consider the following:

- Reading labels and tags: names, addresses, dates, building names, public signs such as "no smoking," "exit").
- Writing basic information: your name, address and telephone number.
- Recognizing the letters of the alphabet or symbols used frequently in a syllabary or character language.

- Reading commonly encountered messages or phrases: menu items, schedules, timetables, maps, signs indicating hours of operation, traffic regulations.
- Reading simple printed material: posters and flyers, simple instructions or directions, newspaper headlines and story titles.
- Writing simple instructions or answers: an invitation, directions to your house, answers on government forms or applications.
- Reading simple paragraphs: letters, invitations, short newspaper or magazine articles, newspaper advertisements.

CULTURAL APPROPRIATENESS

As one learns a language, particularly when immersed in a cultural setting, one learns not only words, sentences, and language structures, but also the customs, values, and beliefs of a people. How people do things, what is more important or less important, and how people relate to each other are reflected in language as well as in actions.

A fifth approach to assessing your language needs and setting your language goals is that of cultural appropriateness. How well does your language use reflect the cultural milieu of the country? We have addressed **survival language** (Can you conduct yourself appropriately in meeting your basic needs: can you ask directions, buy food, tip, use transportation and the telephone, purchase and bargain, do routine banking, etc.?) and **routine relations** (Can you act appropriately in common relations with others: make polite requests, accept and refuse invitations, offer and receive gifts, offer appropriate greetings and leave-takings, make introductions, apologize, express your wants and needs, etc.?).

Equally important to your language learning are the concepts, behavior, and language that are rooted in a society's culture. Consider the following as key components of your language learning program.

Nonverbal cues: Can you respond to (and send) appropriate nonverbal messages that accompany the spoken language? For example, do you understand and correctly use gestures, facial reactions, body stance or movement, distance and closeness, hesitation or avoidance?

Common taboos: Do you recognize common rules of etiquette, taboos, and sensitive topics and situations? For example, are you sensitive to proper public interaction between men and women, elderly and young, authorities and citizens; appropriate ways to eat, dress, conduct oneself in public; topics you shouldn't discuss, questions you shouldn't ask, or places you shouldn't go?

Situational differences: Are you able to modify your language to fit different social situations? For example, do you know appropriate language for informal situations versus formal events; social class or position differences that require different language use, words of supplication or respect; professional gatherings and discussions that require specialized vocabulary and concepts?

Culturally related humor: As your language grows, you will be able to join in language-based humor. Can you understand (and then deliver) common jokes, puns, and wordplay; humor based on regional dialects, foreign accents and stereotypes; humor based on political and comic strip figures?

Allusions: Can you pick out and respond to indirect references to historical and current events, literary references? Can you understand and use idioms, proverbs, folktales?

SEASON THESE HINTS WITH A DASH OF PRACTICALITY

Immersion in another culture and language is no simple task. One doesn't suddenly cast off one's cultural self, forswear use of the native tongue, and cloak oneself in a new language.

As a practical matter, your language learning need not consume every minute of every waking hour. You don't fail if you speak English from time to time. In fact, your language learning should include breaks—both from slavish devotion to a single routine and from language learning in general. Do take time to discuss **in English** your cultural experiences with your English-speaking friends. Use your English to explore the meaning of living abroad, your frustrations and joys, your realization of those values and beliefs which make you American.

Our approach here should merely guide your language learning. Some suggestions may suit your learning style less than others. No problem! We advocate no single lock-step program. This approach will work if you follow its general thrust.

In summary, the language-learning potential of living abroad can best be realized if you

1. assiduously seek to interact with host country people **in their language**;

2. take positive, active steps to expand your language ability; and

3. use a host of tools, ideas, and events to practice, practice, practice your target language.

At best, these suggestions should spark practical ideas which mesh with your own personality, your learning needs and learning style, and your time lines.

Seven

Preparation:
Getting a Head Start at Home

Too often, too little time exists to prepare for going overseas. Despite our best plans, word comes at the last minute— "Yes, the job is yours; we need you within the month!" Then follows a helter-skelter dash to complete a thousand tasks. We scribble lists. We work furiously. Even on the final night before departure we find ourselves occupied far into the night. Then, when the plane is in the air, only then, can we relax.

That period between notification and departure is hectic. But it is also exciting. We look forward with anticipation. We study and restudy the atlas, pour through what information we can find about our destination, seek from those who have been there any hint on "what it's like there."

Yet, in anticipation of life abroad, it is easy to overlook a simple, but important fact: besides gaining access to new adventures, you are leaving behind the comfortable and familiar. Preparation for departure means not only packing physical belongings, but tying up emotional loose ends. This process—leave taking—is a key prerequisite to being able to free your energy for the tasks ahead. No matter how pure your intentions, you cannot effectively learn if you are worried about people, things, or ongoing problems you have left behind.

This admonition, easily stated, is difficult to follow. Departure often requires making sure that elderly parents (or adult children) are secure;

that the house, though not yet rented or sold, is in the hands of a competent agent; that the family pets and plants have new homes; that client relationships have been brought to a successful conclusion; that legal affairs have been attended to—a proper will executed, a potential lawsuit resolved; that work projects have been completed or passed on to others.

Leave taking also involves an endless list of details, such as medical exams, inoculations and consultation; travel plans, including tickets, passports and visas, work permits, packing and shipping; anticipation and plans for life abroad, including shopping for clothing and other necessary items. It means making arrangements for possessions—house, car, belongings which may need to be stored or sold; notifying correspondents of your impending address change; ending or changing subscriptions; closing accounts and services; arranging for bills that will come after you leave. And the list goes on, seemingly forever.

For most of us departure means having said appropriate goodbyes to friends and loved ones, having taken time to visit again or drop a note to an ailing relative, having made a last trip to a favorite haunt.

Proper leave taking requires effort, consumes time. When have your efforts been enough? No easy answer exists. We can offer only the recommendation that leave taking become an integral part of predeparture activities.

Finding time to add language learning to your hectic predeparture days is not easily accomplished; yet, despite the myriad tasks to be taken care of and the stress of your schedule, language learning should remain a high priority. It has an immediately practical use: if you can speak a few key phrases the moment you step off that plane, life will be much easier. Beyond that, your ability to work language learning into your predeparture establishes a pattern that enables you to resume your study immediately upon arrival (a period no less hectic than predeparture). By beginning language study immediately upon arrival, you greatly increase the likelihood that you will continue with it.

This final chapter looks at language learning in the context of predeparture preparation and suggests ways to begin your language learning at home, amid the welter of activities.

ENROLL IN A LANGUAGE CLASS

If possible, enroll in a formal language class before you leave the U.S., preferably a full-time immersion program.

Formal classes force you to program definite language learning hours into your schedule. If you are a beginner, and have only a few weeks, formal classes will introduce you to the sounds and structure of the language, teach you a few basic words and sentences, and foster the notion that language learning will be an important part of your daily life in the months to come. If you are more experienced, classes will help polish your skills, and propel you into your new environment

LIVE "ABROAD" AT HOME

In the long run, immersion in a target language-speaking environment is necessary to foster fluency, control of idioms, and the natural rhythm characteristic of those fluent in a second language. But make the most of your resources here at home. In addition to formal language class (or even if you don't have opportunity for formal study because your target language is an uncommon one), begin in situ training by utilizing the rich resource of people from different ethnic backgrounds right here in the United States.

When we think of native speakers of foreign languages in the U.S., we think immediately of Spanish-speaking communities of the West, Southwest, Midwest, Florida, and New York. Cities such as Los Angeles, Miami, San Antonio, Chicago, and New York boast thousands of Spanish-speaking residents. In addition, throughout the nation in small towns in Wisconsin, Michigan, Colorado, and Idaho (most states in fact), we find clusters of Spanish speakers. Many have lived in their communities for generations; others have recently immigrated.

Our nation's linguistic richness by no means ends with Spanish, however. Our largest cities offer enormous language variety—New York, Boston, and Chicago in particular offer a multiethnic richness. Northern Wisconsin has its Germanic and Scandinavian communities, Maine its French population; thousands of Japanese- and Chinese-Americans live in such cities as San Francisco and New York.

Beyond the more widely known concentrations of ethnic communities, however, are a mosaic of peoples in most major American cities. Take Denver, for example, a city not renowned for ethnic diversity. In addition to a sizable Hispanic population, its residents include numerous Vietnamese, Laotian, Cambodian, and H'Mong immigrants, as well as Japanese, Chinese, Korean, German, Italian, French, Palestinian, Ukrainian, Filipino, Greek, and other communities. While many Americans no longer speak the languages of their forefathers, many tens of thousands do. Our melting pot, we find, is more akin to a tossed salad with rich nuggets of clearly identifiable ethnic and language strains than it is to a blended stew.

In any community with native speakers of your target language— and the U.S has many such communities—you have the potential to enlist native speakers as mentors and to conduct wokabaots into language-specific ethnic neighborhoods.

We make two assumptions here: (1) that in such neighborhoods men and women do exist who, if approached properly, will be willing to help local "foreigners" improve their language skills, and (2) that acceptance in such neighborhoods requires a much different attitude and demeanor than normally characterizes majority/minority relations in this country.

You must become learner and respectful outsider. Don't storm into another person's neighborhood asking questions or making demands. Instead, approach neighbors through a gradually expanding network of friends and confidants, just as you would if you were overseas. In the process, you will demonstrate an interest in, an appreciation for, and an acceptance of ways and experiences different from your own. And, you develop friends in abundance.

You may find people who resent such intrusion, just as overseas you may find people who have no love for Americans. But they are the minority of the minority. Them, you leave alone.

The point is, opportunities exist to learn from native speakers. You need not wait until you step off the plane to begin practical, interactive language learning. The in situ approach provides a structure, rationale, and exercises that enable you to begin your language learning in your own backyard.

How do you find mentors in the U.S.? Just as you would overseas: seek them out in their own communities. If you are in formal language classes and if you like the instructor, propose that she work with you as mentor outside the classroom. Or, ask her to help you identify other likely mentors in the community. If such classes don't exist (and you find commercial language programs such as Berlitz too expensive), go into the neighborhoods, meet people, and recruit them. If you don't know the location of a particular ethnic or language group in your neighborhood, use the Yellow Pages, the newspapers, and city hall to find out. Try the following:

1. Identify ethnic churches, associations, stores, restaurants as initial contacts to learn the general location of ethnic communities and/ or to identify people who can introduce you to target language-speaking populations.

2. Read back issues of local newspapers to learn of ethnic groups and ethnic events that might lead you to members of the appropriate target language groups.

3. Identify cultural appreciation, interchange, or study groups likely to have an interest in and knowledge of the appropriate target language groups. These include associations of returned Peace Corps

volunteers, exchange programs such as Sister Cities, and city human relations commissions.

4. Identify individual families. Contact the appropriate offices at a nearby university or college—the foreign student affairs office, language department, and geographic area study programs—to identify individual foreign students, foreign faculty members, and American students with interest in particular countries and languages. Additionally, check your local public schools to see if they keep records of the language backgrounds of their students. (Many schools may not give out specific names. They might, however, be willing to serve as an intermediary. Ask school officials to contact an appropriate family, and have them ask the family to contact you.)

After all, even if you make contact with only one family in your community who speaks your target language, you have opened doors to begin your learning.

5. Look to the free or alternative universities which have sprung up around the country. They offer short, practical courses (usually inexpensive), frequently including languages, foreign travel, and ethnic music, dance, and philosophy.

6. Scour the literature that identifies national and local organizations and interest groups and discusses the history and location of various immigrant groups in the U.S.

Many learners feel a need to supplement in situ approaches with written and audiovisual materials. If you are learning a major world language which is less commonly taught than Spanish and French (such as Russian, Japanese, Chinese, Arabic), abundant materials exist— many from mainline publishers. For many "exotic" languages, written and/or audiovisual materials prepared by the U.S. government can be obtained with relative ease (though with some expense). Yes, materials are readily available in Hungarian, Greek, Fula, Igbo, Swahili, Swedish, Shona, Sinhalese, and dozens of other languages.

Recommended readings on the above suggestions are included in the reference section for this chapter at the end of the book.

GO WOKABAOT IN YOUR OWN BACK YARD

Chapter 5 presents six detailed daily learning cycles for the overseas learner. Let's look at those activities again, but this time from the perspective of using them in the U.S. while you are preparing to go overseas. Working with a formal language instructor or local mentor, use them individually or as supplemental activities to classroom instruction.

Dining Out: Go on a Restaurant Excursion

Dining out is probably the easiest of all exercises to carry out in the U.S.: most cities host dozens of restaurants that specialize in Mexican, French, Italian, Japanese, Chinese, Greek, and German cuisine. Additionally, tucked away in various ethnic neighborhoods of our country's cities are an amazing variety of ethnically diverse cafes and restaurants. Approach eating out as a language activity, as well as a dining experience. Rather than going to a restaurant, ordering in English, having a good time tasting dishes and then forgetting their names, try the following ideas.

Simulate the experience before dining out. Obtain a menu ahead of time. Learn the names of each dish. If you are working with other learners, role-play the dinner. Bring in a checkered tablecloth and candles and pictures of various dishes cut from magazines. Practice ordering and taking orders around the dining room table and serve the pictures on plates to those who order correctly. Practice the experience until all in the group can order for themselves.

Warn the restaurant ahead of time. Ask your teacher or mentor to talk to the manager. Get his approval to direct his staff to speak only in the target language. Ask them to explain the ingredients of particular dishes and instruct you in culturally appropriate table manners. For a special treat, arrange a field trip during a less busy time of the day and get the chef to demonstrate how he makes a particular dish (in the target language, of course).

Visit an international market or ethnic food store. Talk to the owner about different foods. Get him to describe (in the target language) how to prepare certain dishes, explain where his foods come from, how they are used in the homeland.

Hold a cooking class. Prepare a simple meal; describe and demonstrate the preparation (in the target language).

Getting Around: Learn to Follow Directions

The simulations designed to prepare for an overseas wokabaot easily transfer to an American setting.

Map walking. Use a map of the capital city of the country where you will be living. Identify major well-known sites, and practice giving and following directions for getting from site to site. If your mentor or teacher has slides, supplement the finger-walking exercise with slides of each site. As you gain fluency, have your mentor randomly show a slide. In response, you give directions to that site.

Neighborhood visits. Most cities have landmarks commonly recognized as part of the ethnic heritage of particular neighborhoods—a church or cathedral, school, restaurant, food store, club or association meeting house. Use such landmarks as the focal point or destination for a wokabaot which takes you into the neighborhood. Such wokabaots can be group events as well as individual forays. Neighborhood visits make particularly meaningful homework exercises.

Exchanging Money: Handle Foreign Currency

You become familiar with a foreign currency by using it. If possible, obtain some currency from the country to which you are headed. Gather enough to conduct sorting drills, that is, five to ten each of major bills and handfuls of coins. (For major currencies, try the exchange booth at an international airport and/or check foreign exchange brokers in the Yellow Pages to see if your community has an office of an international exchange bank such as Deak International.)

Short of real money, photocopy or draw a reasonable facsimile and run off multiple copies. While copies won't teach you to sense the differences among bills, they do provide the props for making change, counting, and buying exercises. Use the exercises suggested in chapter 5 in your predeparture training.

Practice counting. Try gaming and counting, calendar and physical response drills, and cuisenaire rods.

Exchange money. You can also practice identifying, adding and subtracting, buying and selling exercises.

Practice metric conversion. Ask a high school science teacher or elementary teacher to recommend idea kits, workbooks, and metric lesson plans that you might use. Simply take the basic exercises and conduct them in the target language.

Going Shopping: Play the Vendor/Buyer Roles

Buying is a critical skill in any overseas experience. Fortunately, all you need is a bit of money, real or pretend, and items to buy and sell—trinkets, food, clothing, empty cans and containers.

The principle is simple: set up situations in which you have the opportunity to become both vendor and buyer. Learn to persuade, bargain, count money, ask for and give change, convert money into goods and goods into money. If you are enrolled in a formal language program, encourage the teacher to organize buying and selling exercises that enable practice one-on-one, in triads, or at most, in groups of four.

To supplement the simulated buying/selling practice (using any of the exercises presented in chapter 5) try the following.

Visit an ethnic food store. Pick up specific items as if you were on a scavenger hunt, or simply browse and come back with interesting items.

Attend crafts and special events fairs. Special events fairs offer opportunities to find and bargain for ethnic items. Frequently such fairs are organized around national or ethnic holidays (5 de Mayo; 16 de Septiembre; Bastille Day, etc.). Many cities have international fairs with booths selling products from different countries.

Getting Medical Care: Prepare for Illness

Integrate language learning with your medical care orientation. Each exercise proposed in chapter 5—"finding directions to the nearest pharmacist," "word guess," and "playing doctor"—can be practiced here in the U.S.

Beyond simulation, however, health care can be an excellent vehicle for obtaining help from an ethnic community's medical professionals. Many American hospitals, particularly training hospitals in major cities, employ nurses, physicians, and other health care professionals from other countries. Call upon their expertise.

Design a first aid class. The American Red Cross probably can't help you very much here; they teach a tightly organized English language program based on a standard text and teaching model. But you can call upon native-speaking health professionals to give either short demonstrations on key first aid topics or longer evening or weekend programs.

Learn about home remedies. Call upon the local target language-speaking community to find people familiar with home remedies. Old folks in particular remember the herbs and potions and treatments that have been used traditionally to heal. Organize a session or two with a guest expert.

Eliciting a Definition: Work up a Questioning Exercise

The questioning exercises suggested in chapter 5 elicit information during an ongoing conversation. They can work equally as well in the U.S. as they can in overseas communities. Try them in classroom conversation involving small groups of students, teacher-student discussion, and simulations, or, if you are working alone, with your mentor.

Post Script:
In-Country Training and in Situ Learning

Rejoice if you are among the fortunate overseas travelers who have access to an intensive language study program upon arrival in your country of destination. Not only will your language skills improve, but you will also be freed from the time-consuming tasks of settling in upon arrival. Chances are you will be met at the airport. Housing will be waiting. Your daily schedule will have been planned for you.

If such is your situation, you have an excellent opportunity to begin developing your in situ skills while under the tutelage of your language instructors.

These days, the training program conducted overseas that does not include a homestay with host nationals is a relic of the past. Trainers recognize the importance of mingling with native speakers in an unstructured setting; and several days or a week spent away from the daily grind of the training site with its four to six hours of language training is a welcome relief for staff and trainee alike. Occasional blocks of free time give opportunity to mingle with host country nationals, to sightsee, to relax.

If you are a student in a study abroad program, you will work with native speakers in the classroom. You will be invited to special programs, events, parties that will give you opportunity to converse informally with instructors and others. You will go on field trips that give you time to explore local communities.

Though mastery of in situ techniques will enable you to draw even more from your overseas environment, most training and study abroad programs haven't yet integrated out-of-class activities with the in-class program nearly as effectively as is possible. Even in training programs with high instructor-to-student ratios, in situ techniques offer an entree to one-on-one learning that is impossible to achieve consistently in class.

You should undertake, as supplement to your formal program, the kinds of in situ exercises suggested throughout this book. Supplement your regular program with the following.

1. Arrange to live with a host family during the course of training, if possible. This will immerse you in the language outside the classroom, and provide the milieu for in situ learning with family members.

2. Try evening or weekend home stays with local families.

3. Organize, if one doesn't already exist, a week-long village stay during your training that immerses you in a totally native-speaking environment.

4. Practice in situ techniques on your own beyond the formal curriculum.

5. Introduce, if possible, in situ exercises into the formal class work. Particularly in extended immersion classes, a good program can easily substitute wokabaots for some traditional in-class activities, thereby making in-class preparation more realistic. Enlist other participants and training staff in developing in situ exercises for your program.

At a minimum, add homework assignments that expose you directly to native speakers in the local community, and develop in situ exercises that help you get the most out of field trips, excursions, or other planned out-of-class events.

To summarize, the day will arrive when classes end and you are on your own. No matter how effective your language training program is, eventually you will leave the program to become an independent, self-directed learner. No program will prepare you so well that you have nothing further to learn.

If you develop your in situ learning skills during your formal program, your transition from classroom student to individual learner will be much the easier.

Supplementary
Reading

The Whole World Guide to Language Learning is a self-contained learning program. It provides the essential tools to develop and carry out your own language learning effort. For readers who may have access to good research libraries and who want supplementary reading, we have compiled readings for each chapter. The following references are arranged by topic and include page references to facilitate follow-up research. Full citations are listed in the bibliography.

Chapter 1 — Settling in: Where Do I Go from Here?

The Learning Cycle Approach. See the suggested readings after chapters 2-5 of this book.

Culture and Language. For an introductory, easy-to-read discussion, see Kohls' *Survival Kit for Overseas Living*. Chapters 2-9 (pages 3-34) discuss the cultural heritage of being an American, and chapters 11-20 (pages 37-73) discuss cross-cultural living. The classic work on this subject is Hall's *The Silent Language*. See especially chapters 8 and 9, pages 165-209.

Chapter 2 — Independence: Creating and Using a Daily Learning Cycle

The Learning Cycle. Larson's *Guidelines for Barefoot Language Learning*, pages 77-100, offers a summary. Larson and Smalley's *Becoming Bilingual*, pages 158-89, explains the concept in more detail. Brewster and Brewster's *Language Acquisition Made Practical*, pages 13-103, demonstrates a one-week learning cycle.

Study Topics. *Language Acquisition Made Practical*, pages 107-9, suggests topics, and pages 137-220 discuss them in more detail. *Guidelines for Barefoot Language Learning*, pages 137-220, includes two hundred situations which can be the basis for planning wokabaots, and *Becoming Bilingual* includes an excellent discussion of advanced learning situations, pages 339-86.

Moran's *Lexicarry*, pages 102-18, provides useful word lists; the *Berlitz [...] for Travellers* series lists survival language terms and phrases.

Drilling Techniques. Clark's *Language Teaching Techniques*, pages 63-116, offers thirteen drills in mini lesson plan form; they are simple, clear, and practical. See *Becoming Bilingual*, pages 141-57 and 226-90, for a broad range of drills. Amy Chipping's chapter in *Language Learner's Field Guide*, pages 307-17, offers examples and a bibliography of sources.

Practice Techniques. Chapter 6 of this book offers techniques adapted from Engleberg's *An Expanded Collection of Language Informant Techniques*. See also Freeman's pamphlet, *101+ Ways to Stimulate Conversation in a Foreign Language*, and pages 5-62 in *Language Teaching Techniques* for additional suggestions.

Chapter 3 — Goals: Benchmarks for Evaluation

Goal Setting. Mager's classic, *Preparing Instructional Objectives*, can be read quickly and effortlessly; see also Gronlund's *Stating Objectives for Classroom Instruction*, pages 14-22, on specific learning outcomes and his checklist for objectives, pages 71-72.

Proficiency Scales. James, *Foreign Language Proficiency in the Classroom and Beyond*, pages 165-72, presents the ACTFL/ETS scale and in Appendix B, page 173, reprints the FSI scale. A fuller treatise of the ACTFL/ETS scale, including proficiencies in French, German, and Spanish, are included in the ACTFL *Provisional Proficiency Guidelines*. Byrnes and Canale's *Defining and Developing Proficiency* updates the ACTFL/ETS scale (pages 15-24) and discusses research and implementation needs.

Brewster and Brewster, *Language Acquisition Made Practical*, Appendix A, pages 369-76, offers a self-assessment checklist. Other checklists are offered in Fantini's *Cross-Cultural Orientation*, pages 23-38 of Appendix I, "Getting the Whole Picture," and Oskarsson's *Approaches to Self-Assessment in Foreign Language Learning*, Appendixes 1-5, pages 37-47.

Chapter Four — Community: Utilizing the Living Classroom

Community Study Ideas. Darrow and Palmquist's *Trans-Cultural Study Guide* contains hundreds of questions you can ask to guide your understanding of any community or country; see pages 20-153. See Larson and Smalley, *Becoming Bilingual*, pages 346-53, for suggestions on understanding neighborhoods and rural communities, and Larson's *Guidelines for Barefoot Language Learning* for his discussion of circles of helpers: "Resources," pages 65-67, and "Use What You Learn," pages 89-94. "Getting the Picture," part 3 (pages 24-53) of Fantini's *Cross-Cultural Orientation* offers a simple framework for community analysis. For a more thorough discussion on community, see Sanders' *The Community: An Introduction to a Social System* or Warren's *Studying Your Community*, two sociological classics. While they discuss the American community, both give a broad-based view that can help you compare the community of your own upbringing to the one you live in abroad. For a classical anthropological text (from a British viewpoint), read *Notes and Queries on Anthropology* by the Royal Anthropological Institution.

Cross-Cultural Cues. Review Kohls' *Survival Kit for Overseas Living*, pages 17-34, for hints on cross-cultural interaction. Additionally, country-specific information is essential to your understanding and living overseas. Check the following to see if your country is included among them: (1) *Culturgram Series*: four-page briefs on culture, language, and the people of eighty-one nations, Center for International Studies, Brigham Young University, Provo, UT 84602 (sold also in a two-volume set as *Culturgrams: The Nations Around Us* [Vol. I—North and South America and Western and Eastern Europe; Vol. II—Middle East, Asia, Africa, and the Pacific], available from Intercultural Press, Yarmouth, ME 04096; (2) *Post Reports*: a pamphlet series by the State Department (available from the Government Printing Office) to introduce new diplomats to their country of assignment, ranging from eleven to fifty-nine pages and covering ninety-three countries; (3) *Background Notes*: a series of short pamphlets by the State Department (also available from the Government Printing Office) with information on the land, people, economy, foreign relations, and U.S. policy of nearly 160 countries; (4) *Country Studies*: 106 volumes published by the Government Printing Office (formerly known as "Area Handbooks") which describe and analyze the economic, military, political, cultural, and social systems and institutions of the subject country. Bound volumes, they range from 185 to 882 pages and each includes an extensive bibliography; (5) *Updates*: a series of volumes which orient the new resident to different countries. Each is approximately 110 pages long and deals with practical concerns of living in the country under study (available from Intercultural Press).

Working with a Mentor. For other discussion of mentors, see "Learning a Foreign Language from an Informant," pages 58-85, in Nida's *Learning a Foreign Language*. For a view of the informant in linguistic research, read "The Language Informant," pages 20-44, in Samarin's *Field Linguistics*.

Working with Monolingual Mentors. There are four short articles in Healey's *Language Learner's Field Guide* which discuss language learning techniques in situations where there are no English speakers. See pages 267-84.

Chapter Five — Plans: The Road to Language Survival

Each individual lesson plan in chapter 5 ends with a one-paragraph mini-bibliography, which includes the key reference items for that lesson plan.

Chapter Six — Techniques and Topics: Where Do I Go When the Pavement Ends?

Learning Techniques. The twelve mini-lessons were adapted from Gary Engelberg's booklet, *An Expanded Collection of Language Informant Techniques* (written for the Peace Corps Regional Training Office in Dakar, Senegal, and reprinted by the Peace Corps Office of Training and Program Support, Washington, DC). Jerald and Clark's *Experiential Language Teaching Techniques* presents twenty-eight minilessons designed to involve learners in their local communities, and Clark's *Language Teaching Techniques*, pages 5-62, offers similar exercises; both are presented in a style similar to the mini-lessons in this chapter. For other suggestions, see Freeman's pamphlet, *101+ Ways to Stimulate Conversation in a Foreign Language*. Although it does not include specific exercises, the pamphlet by Kraft and Kraft, *Where Do I Go From Here?* is a good source of encouragement for language learners.

Situations. The Berlitz *[...] for Travellers* series offers specific, common examples of survival language. Brewster and Brewster's *Language Acquisition Made Practical*, pages 107-08, summarizes useful discussion topics.

Linguistic Approaches. Larson and Smalley's *Becoming Bilingual* discusses how to approach a language, pages 107-40 and provides help in pronunciation, pages 190-225. Larson's *Guidelines for Barefoot Language Learning*, pages 110-326, offers two hundred suggested language skills. *Language Acquisition Made Practical*, pages 247-312, addresses pronunciation. Rubin and Thompson's *How to be a More Successful Language Learner*, pages 67-90, offers suggestions based on linguistic knowledge. See the ACTFL/ETS *Provisional Proficiency Guidelines* for hints on useful skills identified by professional language teachers.

Expressions and Word lists. Moran's *Lexicarry* consists of thousands of simple drawings useful for eliciting words from a mentor; it also contains extensive word lists. The Berlitz series offers a number of specific, practical usages. Healey's *Language Learner's Field Guide*, pages 460-64, includes a list entitled "Useful Expressions." *Becoming Bilingual*, pages 262-90, has a chapter on techniques for expanding vocabulary.

Cultural Concerns. *Becoming Bilingual*, pages 291-311, casts language learning into its cultural context and discusses the idea of expanding one's understanding of the variety which exists in a language, pages 358-86. Hall's *The Silent Language* is a good general survey of the notion of nonverbal cues. The *Provisional Proficiency Guidelines* includes a separate section which discusses cultural appropriateness of language usage at each ability level.

Learning Resources. Look at *How to Be a More Successful Language Learner*, pages 93-108, and *Becoming Bilingual*, pages 88-106. See also "Learning a Foreign Language from a Teacher," pages 39-57, in *Learning a Foreign Language*.

General Hints. *Language Learner's Field Guide* offers two useful articles: Healey's "Language Learning," pages 285-96, and Pike's "Language Learning in Relation to Focus," pages 297-306.

Chapter Seven — Preparation: Getting a Head Start at Home

We are not aware of other sources that relate in situ techniques to foreign language learning in the United States. For discussion of related ideas, however, see the following:

Use of Mentors. Fantini's suggestions in *Beyond the Language Classroom* for involving foreign exchange students in language classrooms apply to American student and community mentors: pages 20-49 contain classroom-related suggestions, pages 71-117 suggest ways in which students may learn from the community. See pages 129-34 of Gaies' *Peer Involvement in Language Learning* for effects of peer teaching, and pages 99-128 for ideas on setting up peer-teaching programs.

Identifying Mentors in the U.S. A booklet by The President's Council for

International Youth Exchange, *One Friendship at a Time; Your Guide to International Youth Exchange*, describes several organizations involved in exchange programs; many have local chapters or offices throughout the U.S. The Peace Corps (1990 K Street, N.W., Washington, DC 20526; tel. 800-424-8580) can refer you to local recruitment offices which are in touch with groups of returned volunteers. Many cities have human relations commissions (or their equivalent) which handle liaison with ethnic minority communities, as well as such organizations as Sister Cities. Information on ethnic groups throughout the U.S. can be found in books by Bernardo, *The Ethnic Almanac*; Wasserman and Kennington, *Ethnic Information Sources of the United States*; and Wynar, *Encyclopedic Directory of Ethnic Organizations in the United States*.

Resources on Specific Languages. See the Center for Applied Linguistics, *Foreign Service Institute Language Teaching Materials*; National Audiovisual Center, *A List of Audiovisual Materials Produced by the United States Government for Foreign Language Instruction*; and Johnson, et. al., *A Survey of Materials for the Study of Uncommonly Taught Languages*.

Visiting Ethnic Communities in the U.S. Petronio's "Tours of the Community As Part of the Conversation Class" and Goldstein's "Vamos al Barrio: Presenting Spanish in Its Primary Context through Field Trips" suggest activities when taking students into neighborhoods. Jerald and Clark's book, *Experiential Language Teaching Techniques*, includes twenty-eight short, practical lesson plans to help students learn outside the classroom.

Overseas Orientation. Cassidy's *Taking Students Abroad* follows the overseas study program from inception through recruitment, planning, fund-raising, preparation, to post-trip evaluation. See pages 77-93 for orientation suggestions. Fantini's workbook, *Cross-Cultural Orientation*, presents the Experiment in International Living approach. Predeparture orientation exercises are included on pages 7-51. Pages 73-99 offer suggestions for those who conduct orientation programs.

Annotated
Bibliography

The Whole World Guide to Language Learning is a book for language learners. We assume that most readers have neither access to nor interest in reading arcane articles about language learning. For those who wish additional information, however, the following bibliography introduces you to the literature.

Continuing Information

The following are sources for continuing information on second language learning. Look to them for future publications.

ACTFL (The American Council on the Teaching of Foreign Languages): 579 Broadway, Hastings-on-Hudson, NY 10706. Publishes *Foreign Language Annals*, brochures, and books on language. ACTFL materials give the mainstream academic orientation rather than self-directed learning; good for contrast.

Barefootnotes: CMS Publishing, Inc., 2325 Endicott St. #27, St. Paul, MN 55114. Four-page bimonthly by Donald Larson with hints on cross-cultural living and language learning.

ERIC Clearinghouse on Languages and Linguistics: Center for Applied Linguistics, 3520 Prospect St, NW, Washington, DC 20007. Source of books, monographs, computer searches, minibibliographies, and information sheets on language learning.

NASILP (National Association of Self-Instructional Language Programs): Center for Critical Languages, Humanities Building, Box 38, Temple University, Philadelphia, PA 19122. Organization geared to helping college institutions develop and maintain self-instructional academic programs.

References Noted

Thousands of articles and books exist on second language learning. We make no pretense of having surveyed the literature to identify everything available. The following, included in the reference section for individual chapters, are of interest to self-directed language learners.

American Council on the Teaching of Foreign Languages
   1982   *Provisional Proficiency Guidelines.* Hastings-on-Hudson, NY: the ACTFL. Language learning goals and proficiency standards.

Batchelder, Donald, and Elizabeth G. Warner
   1977   *Beyond Experience: The Experiential Approach to Cross-Cultural Education.* Brattleboro, VT: The Experiment Press. Includes the Experiment's language assessment form.

Berlitz
   various dates
            [Latin-American Spanish][French][etc.] for Travellers. New York: Macmillan. Survival vocabulary in translation.

Bernardo, Stephanie
   1981   *The Ethnic Almanac.* New York: Dolphin Books. Potpourri of references to American ethnic groups.

Brewster, E. Thomas, and Elizabeth S. Brewster
   1976   *Language Acquisition Made Practical.* Pasadena, CA: Lingua House. LAMP offers a useful, practical orientation to self-directed language learning. It is based on Larson and Smalley's Learning Cycle and is written simply and with a minimum of jargon. It suggests study topics beyond the initial explanation of the learning cycle, as well as more technical discussion of language drills and pronunciation. LAMP is chock-full of clever, entertaining line drawings, cartoons, and quips to liven it up. For all that, LAMP is a jumble: you can pull lots of things from it (and you should), but it doesn't provide the clear, precise instruction you need as a field-based learner.

Byrnes, Heidi, and Michael Canale (eds.)
   1987   *Defining and Developing Proficiency: Guidelines, Implementations, and Concepts.* Lincolnwood, IL: National Textbook Company. Updates and discusses ACTFL/ETS proficiency scale and its implementation.

Cassidy, Maggie Brown
   1984   *Taking Students Abroad: A Guide for Teachers.* Portland, ME: J. Weston Walch. How to plan, organize, and implement a study abroad program.

Center for Applied Linguistics
nd   *Foreign Service Institute Language Teaching Materials.* (ERIC Computer Search #390). Washington, DC: Center for Applied Linguistics. A list of materials on numerous languages.

Clark, Raymond C.
1985   *Potluck: Exploring American Foods and Meals.* Brattleboro, VT: Pro Lingua Associates. Set of short readings and follow-up questions on preparing, serving, and eating food.

1980   *Language Teaching Techniques.* Brattleboro, VT: Pro Lingua Associates. A set of short, practical language drills and exercises presented in a minilesson format.

Darrow, Ken, and Brad Palmquist (eds.)
1977   *Trans-Cultural Study Guide.* Stanford: Volunteers in Asia. Questions and topics for cross-cultural understanding.

Engelberg, Gary
1976   *An Expanded Collection of Language Informant Techniques.* Washington, DC: United States Peace Corps. Practical hints on language learning.

Fantini, Alvino E. (ed.)
1984a   *Beyond the Language Classroom: A Guide for Language Teachers.* Brattleboro, VT: The Experiment in International Living. Manual for utilizing foreign exchange students in the foreign language classroom.

1984b   *Cross-Cultural Orientation: A Guide for Leaders and Educators.* Brattleboro, VT: The Experiment in International Living. Includes practical hints on understanding an overseas community.

Freeman, G. Ronald
nd   *101+ Ways to Stimulate Conversation in a Foreign Language.* Hastings-on-Hudson, NY: ACTFL Materials Center. Practical hints; classroom oriented.

Gaies, Stephen J.
1985   *Peer Involvement in Language Learning.* Orlando, FL: Harcourt Brace Jovanovich, Inc. Review of programs using peer teaching; suggests how to set up such programs.

Goldstein, Nina White
1986   "Vamos al Barrio: Presenting Spanish in Its Primary Context through Field Trips," *Foreign Language Annals* 19:3 (May), 209-217. Detailed plans for taking students on field trips into Hispanic neighborhoods.

Gronlund, Norman E.
1985   *Stating Objectives for Classroom Instruction (3rd ed.).* New York: Macmillan Publishing Company. Manual on writing educational objectives.

Hall, Edward T.
   1959   *The Silent Language.* Garden City, NY: Doubleday & Company, Inc. The classic work on nonverbal communication.

Healey, Alan (ed.)
   1975   *Language Learner's Field Guide.* Ukarumpa, Papua New Guinea: Summer Institute of Linguistics. In three parts this volume offers (1) an introduction to settling into a community; (2) a set of forty units designed as day-to-day learning activities; and (3) a set of readings. Each unit suggests learning topics (e.g., observing sickness and health) and several activities (e.g., "track a discussion"), and recommends particular grammatical points for each topic. The articles offer helpful tips on such topics as working with monolingual speakers, eliciting vocabulary and language structure, handling cross-cultural stress, taking notes, filing information, keeping track of your progress, etc. The work relies heavily on understanding and working with grammar.

Holec, Henri
   1979   *Autonomy and Foreign Language Learning.* Oxford: Pergamon Press. Short theoretical look at self-directed language learning, with practical implications.

James, Charles J. (ed.)
   1985   *Foreign Language Proficiency in the Classroom and Beyond.* Lincolnwood, IL: National Textbook Company. Language learning goals and proficiency standards.

Jerald, Michael, and Raymond C. Clark
   1983   *Experiential Language Teaching Techniques.* Brattleboro, VT: Pro Lingua Associates. Twenty-eight short, practical lesson plans designed to help students continue language learning outside the classroom.

Johnson, Dora E., et al.
   1976   *A Survey of Materials for the Study of the Uncommonly Taught Languages.* Orlando, FL: Harcourt Brace Jovanovich International. Seven-volume annotated list of materials including dictionaries, grammars, readers, and teaching materials in hundreds of languages.

Kohls, L. Robert
   1984   *Survival Kit for Overseas Living (rev. ed.)* Yarmouth, ME: Intercultural Press, Inc. Practical hints on cross-cultural living.

Kraft, Marguerite E., and Charles H. Kraft
   1966   *Where Do I Go from Here?: A Handbook for Continuing Language Study in the Field.* Washington, DC: United States Peace Corps. Pamphlet which encourages continued language learning for Peace Corps volunteers. Includes practical hints.

Kunz, John
   1965   *Modern Mathematics Made Meaningful.* New Rochelle, NY: Cuisenaire Company of America. Handbook with exercises for using cuisenaire rods.

Lafayette, Robert C., and Lorraine A. Strasheim
   1984   "The Standard Sequence and the Non-Traditional Methodologies," *Foreign Language Annals* 17:6 (December): 567-74. Discussion of recent language teaching strategies and their implications for the classroom.

Larson, Donald N.
   1984   *Guidelines for Barefoot Language Learning.* St. Paul, MN: CMS Publishing, Inc. The first third of Larson's book introduces language learning and lays out a process based on the learning cycle for directing one's own learning. The remaining two-thirds is a set of two hundred situations meant to serve as the basis for specific daily language-learning activities. Larson's approach to the learning cycle is very useful; his words are positive, encouraging, and lay out the idea succinctly and clearly. However, the author uses a vocabulary of his own devising which can be confusing to the beginning language learner (e.g., topics such as "primary faceworking," "seamworking," etc.). Nor does the book offer the nitty-gritty instructions necessary for its readers to know how to use the material.

Larson, Donald N., and William A. Smalley
   1984   *Becoming Bilingual (2nd. ed.).* Lanham, MD: University Press of America. This is a reprint of the 1972 edition. It is an excellent resource for the field-based learner. It explains the learning cycle approach, gives practical hints on self-directed learning, provides numerous examples of drills, interesting language and cultural faux pax, anecdotes, numerous references. It reviews and critiques second language learning theories and addresses how people learn languages. It is a textbook rather than a field manual: one can't sit down with it and develop a program of action. It remains an excellent reference work to look to for follow-up study, explanation, and learning hints.

Liskin-Gasparro, Judith E.
   1984   "The ACTFL Proficiency Guidelines: Gateway to Testing and Curriculum," *Foreign Language Annals* 17:5 (October): 475-89. Language learning goals and proficiency standards.

Logan, Gerald E.
   1973   *Individualized Foreign Language Learning: An Organic Process.* Rowley, MA: Newbury House Publishers, Inc. Text on one approach to language teaching.

Mager, Robert F.
   1962   *Preparing Instructional Objectives.* Belmont, CA: Fearon Publishers. Easy-to-read workbook on writing educational objectives.

Moran, Patrick R.
   1984   *Lexicarry: An Illustrated Vocabulary-builder for Second Languages.* Brattleboro, VT: Pro Lingua Associates. Thousands of drawings without text; useful for generating discussion with a mentor. Also includes extensive word lists.

National Audiovisual Center
nd   *A List of Audiovisual Materials Produced by the United States Govern-
       ment for Foreign Language Instruction.* Washington, DC: National
       Audiovisual Center, General Services Administration, National Ar-
       chives and Records Service. Pricelist for audiocassetts for thirty-five
       languages.

Nida, Eugene A.
1957   *Learning a Foreign Language.* New York: Friendship Press. Written first
       for missionaries but not limited to their needs, Nida's book is a good
       introduction to field-based language learning. The first half of Nida's
       book offers many practical study hints. It reads easily, primarily
       because of its practical orientation, the numerous examples of language
       use from several nonwritten languages, and the lack of technical
       linguistic jargon. The latter half, dealing with pronunciation, syntax, and
       grammar, is more technical. *Learning a Foreign Language* adds insight
       and ideas to the learning process. It does not, however, present a
       systematic method by which to organize one's language learning.

Oskarsson, Mats
1978   *Approaches to Self-assessment in Foreign Language Learning.* Oxford:
       Pergamon Press. Short work on self-assessment; includes different
       formats for evaluation.

Petronio, Vivetta G.
1985   "Tours of the Community As Part of the Conversation Class," *Foreign
       Language Annals* 18:2 (April), 157-59. Short paper suggesting ways to
       include field trips in foreign language classes.

President's Council for International Youth Exchange
1983   *One Friendship at a Time: Your Guide to International Youth Exchange.*
       Washington, DC: The Consortium for International Citizen Exchange.
       Pamphlet describing various exchange programs.

Rollins, Nicholas
1983   *American Express International Traveler's Pocket Dictionary and Phrase
       Book.* New York: Simon & Schuster. Traveler's phrase book.

Royal Anthropological Institution
1951   *Notes and Queries on Anthropology.* London: Routledge and Kegan
       Paul, Ltd. Classical anthropological field guide.

Rubin, Joan, and Irene Thompson
1982   *How to Be a More Successful Language Learner.* Boston: Heinle &
       Heinle. Practical hints; oriented to supplementing a classroom ap-
       proach.

Samarin, William J.
1967   *Field Linguistics.* New York: Holt, Rinehart and Winston. Text for
       students doing linguistic studies in overseas societies.

Sanders, Irvin T.
  1966 *The Community: An Introduction to a Social System.* New York: The
        Roland Press Company. Presents a systematic approach to community
        study, based on American communities.

Stevick, Earl W.
  1980 *Teaching Languages: A Way and Ways.* Rowley, MA: Newbury House
        Publishers, Inc. Explanation of several second language methodolo-
        gies.

Warren, Roland L.
  1955 *Studying Your Community.* New York: Russell Sage Foundation. A
        basic text on community study, based on American communities.

Wasserman, Paul, and Alice Kennington
  1983 *Ethnic Information Sources of the United States (2nd ed).* Detroit: Gale
        Research Company. Two-volume reference work with much informa-
        tion.

Werner, David
  1977 *Where There Is No Doctor: A Village Health Care Handbook.* Palo Alto,
        CA: Hesperian Foundation. Layman's manual for personal health care.

Wynar, Lubomyr R.
  1975 *Encyclopedic Directory of Ethnic Organizations in the United States.*
        Littleton, CO: Libraries Unlimited, Inc. Short summaries of 1,475 ethnic
        organizations.

Index